THE INDEX OF COINCIDENCE

WITH PERSONAL NOTE TO WILLIAM F. FRIEDMAN

By HOWARD H. CAMPAIGNE

NIMBLE BOOKS LLC: THE AI LAB FOR BOOK-LOVERS

~ FRED ZIMMERMAN, EDITOR ~

Humans and AI making books richer, more diverse, and more surprising.

PUBLISHING INFORMATION

(c) 2024 Nimble Books LLC
ISBN: 978-1-60888-253-3

v21.0.0-VernorVinge
commit 17999454f9406f4cab649b0be577bee654406b77

PUBLISHER'S NOTES

This annotated edition illustrates the capabilities of the AI Lab for Book-Lovers to add context and ease-of-use to manuscripts. It includes several types of abstracts, building from simplest to more complex: a breakdown by semantic structure; a selection of most important passages; and notable passages and nutshell summaries for each page.

CONTENTS

ANNOTATIONS

TLDR (THREE WORDS):

Coincidence, Codebreaking, Statistics.

ELI5

Imagine you have a big box of letters, and you want to know if someone just threw them in randomly or if they arranged them in a special way. The Index of Coincidence is like a detective tool that helps us figure that out by counting how often the same letters appear together. It's like a game of finding matching pairs!

SCIENTIFIC-STYLE ABSTRACT

This pamphlet discusses the Index of Coincidence (I.C.), a statistical tool used in cryptanalysis to determine the randomness of text and the similarity between different texts. It explores various applications of the I.C., including identifying messages encrypted with the same key, determining the overlap between messages in depth, and assessing the roughness of single text samples. The document also delves into the theoretical underpinnings of the I.C., explaining its expected values for different languages and polygraphic comparisons. It further elucidates the concept of standard deviation as a measure of the significance of I.C. deviations from expected values. The pamphlet examines the Cross I.C. as a correlation measure and provides a detailed example of using the I.C. to align secondary alphabets into a primary one for deciphering Vigenere ciphertexts. Finally, it addresses the I.C. of modular sums, mixed texts, and rectangular arrays, concluding with a discussion of the relationship between Chi-Square and the I.C.

SEMANTIC STRUCTURE

- **Pamphlet (Cryptanalysis)**: Explores the Index of Coincidence (I.C.) for codebreaking.

MOST IMPORTANT PASSAGES

Passage 1:

"Coincidence" as the term is used here may be defined as a recurrence of a letter in the same place, or in a corresponding place, as when two texts are lined up one under the other, letter for letter. Mathematical evaluation assists the cryptanalyst first in preparing his material for attack, and later in the actual attack itself. (Page 1)

Rationale: This passage sets the stage for the entire pamphlet, introducing the core concept of "coincidence" and its crucial role in cryptanalysis.

Passage 2:

The ratio of the number of coincidences to the number of coincidences expected in random text is called the "index of coincidence", and is abbreviated as "I.C." or "δ". (Page 2)

Rationale: This defines the I.C. mathematically, providing the foundational formula for understanding the rest of the document.

Passage 3:

The process just described is a basic one, and variations of it will always be useful to the cryptanalyst. (Page 7)

Rationale: This statement highlights the practical importance and adaptability of the I.C. for various cryptanalytic tasks.

PAGE-BY-PAGE SUMMARIES

NOTABLE PASSAGES

BODY-5   *"Mathematical evaluation assists the cryptanalyst first in preparing his material for attack, and later in the actual attack itself. It assists specifically in answering the following questions. 1) How much like random, or how different from random, is this text? 2) How similar are these texts? 3) How significant is this variation from random? 4) How significant is this similarity?"*

BODY-6   *Text which appears to meet these conditions is sometimes described as "flat". Text which fails to be random in some way is called "rough".*

BODY-7   *"Finally, there are 66,930 chances in 1,000,000 (the sum of the chances for the individual letters) of both letters' being the same letter in a chance selection. Therefore, if we select many pairs of plain text letters, the average number of identical letters to be expected 'in the long run' will be 6.69% (about 1/15) of the total number of possible coincidences."*

BODY-8   *In addition to the simple monographic Index of Coincidence, there are occasions when the digraphic I. C. (i2), trigraphic I. C. (,1), tetragraphic I. C. (,.), pentagraphic I. C. (,6), etc., can be used to advantage. They are derived from the normal digraphic (trigraphic, etc.) frequency tables in the manner indicated in section I.*

BODY-11   *There are 14 coincidences in 220 pairs of letters. N = 220 = 8.46 coincidences expected. IC = 1.66 (almost normal for English). These two messages probably are in the same key (and actually proved to be). Note that there are no repeated digraphs or trigraphs. Note also that coincidences are well spread out.*

BODY-12   *If the text is not flat but proportions Pi. P2, ... , Po of letters, then there are $f_i = P_i M$ occurrences of the i th letter. In the course of our counting we will compare every letter with every other, so that the i th letter will give rise to f_i ($f2-1$) coincidences.*

BODY-13   *The error in using 'Y (usually more convenient) in place of a is*

I ?-I ~~?1 ~- I

(17)

This error is always positive, that is, 'Y is an over-estimat.e of a.

The error is smaller for larger values of 'Y, or larger values of M.

Notice that 'Y is a measure of the shape of the distribution only, and is independent of the

sample size, as

(18)

since $f1 = p1M$.

But a does depend on the sample size M, which is a desirable characteristic, since random roughness is usually present in small samples.

BODY-14   The index of coincidence indicates that a monoalphabetic substitution was employed.

BODY-15   To estimate the significance of IJ, we refer to (12), where the denominator is the expected number of incidences in flat text, and the numerator is the number found. The standard deviation of IJ is a (IJ) = .j'~~~~l)' see Appendix III. That is, in the first example of the previous section IJ=1.76, and a(IJ) = ./17~ ~ 2: 72 =.04. Thus IJ is:: =19 standard deviations above the value expected from a flat universe. In the second example of the previous section, IJ = 1.49 and a(IJ) = ./2~:6; i~ 5 12s=·

BODY-16   The tables of Appendix VI enable one to estimate the significance of a sigmage as a probability. If a probability Prob (S <;S,) is not in the table of Appendix VI then the entry P [c 21 , ~ l is a good approximation, b=Sov2(e-l)+e-l, where P(x,a) is the Poisson cumulative function, tabulated in the Cryptanalyst's Manual, Section 6-1, Table II, published by the National Security Agency. If the probability is too small even for the Poisson tables then it is closely approximated by Prob (S :Sk) :::;:: k! where a= 2e.

BODY-17   The function E can be used as a measure of correlation between two distributions.

BODY-22   "To prove correct alignment: The index for the given relative position of two distributions must be higher than for all other positions, with no close second. The index should be 1.50 or higher (preferably 1.73 or higher). There must be only one acceptable alignment."

BODY-23   "When strips are properly aligned, the indicators show the relative positions of these letters in the cipher component. The student is advised to prepare strips for himself and follow these processes. First, match T against B. As no two letters can occupy the same position in the cipher component, begin by setting the T indicator at No. 2 on the B master alphabet. Count the coincidences. Next, slide T to No. 3, and count the coincidences. Continue this process to No. 26, and record the successive numbers of coincidences in tabular form."

BODY-24   The most certain combination is T (1)-N (5), and there is no doubt as to its correctness. This located "N" relative to "T" in the cipher component, and allows us to consolidate their frequencies.

BODY-25   "The master distribution (of 100 letters or more) should approximate a normal frequency distribution and will give a standard to which all the other distributions can be referred. Hereafter, variations in the highest index of coincidence will be due entirely to letter distribution of the various distributions themselves."

BODY-26   "The cipher component has now been completely recovered. The process described above has actually built up the complete squared-cipher-table of a modified Vigenere table. We have written down the cipher component rather than the complete square table merely to save time and effort."

BODY-27   The chi-square test is a standard statistic for comparing two distributions. It is more flexible than the I.C. and its use has been described in many places. It is also *more tricky than the I.C., its very flexibility making it hard for a beginner to use intelligently.*

BODY-28   *The material presented here has been collected in the hope of helping the cryptanalyst with his decision problems. More on this fundamentally sophisticated subject can be found in "Statistics for Cryptology" and "Probability and the Weighing of Evidence" by I. J. Good. Many papers on specific phases of decisions are to be found in the "Collected Papers of Mathematical Cryptology" or in the "Quarterly Summary" of NSA--34.*

BODY-29   *Problem: Some cipher machines have a switch which must be thrown one way to encipher and the other way to decipher. The switch reverses the direction of flow of information through the machine. A certain operator inadvertently uses decipher on his machine in preparing a message, and sends it that way. The recipient is unable to understand it and requests a resend. The operator repeats his operation, using the same setting as before, but with the switch now on encipher.*

BODY-31   *The monographic and digraphic I. C.'s are not independent. For if the probabilities of the individual letters are Pi, Pi, - - -, Po then the expected probability $E(pii)$ of the digraph ij is $P \cdot Pi$. ignoring the cohesion of the language, and for the moment imagining a sample like newspaper which has been cut into little pieces, one letter to a piece, which have been shuffled and arranged in a line. Using this estimate of Pli we get the expected value.*

BODY-35   *Now by definition a $R(f) = E(f^2)-[E(f))^2]$*

BODY-40   *If we take $N \sim l \sim 1$ (Error less than 1% for $N \sim 50$). The above is reasonably accurate and can be tabulated for values of sigmage S without regard for sample size. Values for the above are tabulated by translation from Pearson's Tables of the Incomplete Gamma Function.*

BODY-41   *The distribution of $S(E)$ has the fortunate property of being approximately independent of the sample size. This makes it feasible to tabulate its distribution. The table, each entry of which is the probability of getting a certain sigmage or higher, was made by translating from Pearson's Table of the Incomplete Beta Function by the formula $P[S(E) \sim k] = I1 k.$*

THE
INDEX OF COINCIDENCE

NATIONAL SECURITY AGENCY

THE

INDEX

OF

COINCIDENCE

NATIONAL SECURITY AGENCY

WASHINGTON 25, D. C.

JANUARY 1955

I

ORIGINAL
Reverse (Page II) Blank

THE INDEX OF COINCIDENCE

FOREWORD

This edition is a revision of the paper published in 1946 by the Chief of Naval Operations, which paper was itself a revision of a pamphlet called "Coincidence", first published in 1929, and revised in 1930, 1939, and in 1940 by the Navy Department.

HOWARD H. CAMPAIGNE
Assistant Chief for Research
Office of Research and Development

12 January 1955

25 Sept. 1955

To Mr W. F. Friedman

with appreciation for his scholarly guidance, with affection for his kindly urbanity, and with regret for his no-longer close association.

Howard Campaigne

TABLE OF CONTENTS

APPENDICES

ORIGINAL
Reverse (Page VI) Blank

INTRODUCTION

The subject of this pamphlet is coincidence.

"Coincidence" as the term is used here may be defined as a recurrence of a letter in the same place, or in a corresponding place, as when two texts are lined up one under the other, letter for letter.

Mathematical evaluation assists the cryptanalyst first in preparing his material for attack, and later in the actual attack itself. It assists specifically in answering the following questions.

1) How much like random, or how different from random, is this text?

2) How similar are these texts?

3) How significant is this variation from random?

4) How is significant is this similarity?

I. Simple Monographic Comparison.

When examining cipher text looking for a break the cryptanalyst keeps in mind as a standard for comparison "random" text. This is text which has no meaning or system behind it, in which each letter can appear as often as any other, in which each digraph can appear as often as any other, and generally no significant pattern can appear except in small samples as the result of chance deviations. Text which appears to meet these conditions is sometimes described as "flat". Text which fails to be random in some way is called "rough".

A test has been devised which measures whether two texts are rough in the same way. This test is performed by writing the texts one above the other and counting the occasions for which the same letters come together, such as an E over an E, called a "coincidence". The ratio of the number of coincidences to the number of coincidences expected in random text is called the "index of coincidence", and is abbreviated as I. C. or ι. $\iota = \dfrac{\text{actual coincidences}}{\text{expected coincidences}}$. If the two texts were random then a coincidence would occur once in 26 trials (for a 26 letter alphabet), or 3.85% of the time. If the two texts were English then there would be more coincidences, almost 7%. The percentage found divided by 3.85% is the I. C.

Most European languages have an I. C. of about 2. For random text the I. C. is 1. The expected I. C. for English can be computed as follows:

Take two pages of English text. Make a chance selection from each page.

There are about 130 chances in 1,000 of the first letter's being an "E" (See table following).

There are about 130 chances in 1,000 of the second letter's being an "E".

There are about 16,900 chances in 1,000,000 of both letters' being an "E".

Likewise, there are 8,464 chances in 1,000,000 of both being "T", 6,400 chances in 1,000,000 of both being "N", etc.

Table

Text Letter (Telegraphic Text)	Chances in 1,000 of 1st letter's being this ltr.	Chances in 1,000 of 2nd letter's being this ltr.	Chances in 1,000,000 of both letters' being this letter
E	130	130	16,900
O	75	75	5,625
A	74	74	5,476
I	73	73	5,329
N	80	80	6,400
R	76	76	5,776
S	61	61	3,729
T	92	92	8,464
D	42	42	1,764
H	34	34	1,156
L	36	36	1,296
C	31	31	961
M	25	25	625
U	26	26	676
P	27	27	729
F	28	28	784
G	16	16	256
Y	19	19	361
B	10	10	100
V	15	15	225
W	16	16	256
K	4	4	16
J	2	2	4
Q	2	2	4
X	5	5	25
Z	1	1	1
Any letter	1,000	1,000	66,930

Finally, there are 66,930 chances in 1,000,000 (the sum of the chances for the individual letters) of both letters' being the same letter in a chance selection. Therefore, if we select many pairs of plain text letters, the average number of identical letters to be expected "in the long run" will be 6.69% (about 1/15) of the total number of possible coincidences.

We may call this number the expected coincidences in English text.

The expected I. C. for English (or monoalphabetic cipher text) is $\frac{.0669}{.0385} = 1.73$

The actual I. C. of unknown cipher text may take almost any value but in practice on small samples the range will generally extend from about .80 to about 2.00 (simple monographic Index of Coincidence).

The value of the index of coincidence for a given English text will depend on the distribution of letters in that text. Repetitions in short texts will increase the index of coincidence. Text with few repetitions will give an I. C. approaching the theoretical 1.73. As the expected number of chance coincidences is based on a flat frequency (where each cipher letter is ultimately used the same number of times) any cipher text that differs radically from such frequency distribution will have a correspondingly higher I. C. This is especially noticeable in short cipher texts where the frequencies have not had an opportunity to "flatten out".

The monographic I. C. of English text will increase with small amounts of text to 1.80–2.00 (as compared with the theoretical 1.73) and small amounts of random text will give I. C.'s of 1.10–1.20 (as compared with the theoretical 1.00). The amount of excess attributable to the sample size will be discussed later, under "standard deviation".

For most European languages the expected I. C. is higher than in English, due to the more irregular letter distribution of their normal alphabets, namely:

Language	Expected I. C.
Random text	1.00
English	1.73
Russian	1.77
Italian	1.93
Spanish	1.94
Portuguese	1.94
French	2.02
German	2.04

II. Polygraphic Comparison.

In addition to the simple monographic Index of Coincidence, there are occasions when the digraphic I. C. (ι_2), trigraphic I. C. (ι_3), tetragraphic I. C. (ι_4), pentagraphic I. C. (ι_5), etc., can be used to advantage. They are derived from the normal digraphic (trigraphic, etc.) frequency tables in the manner indicated in section I.

Expected values for the simple digraphic index of coincidence is as follows:

Language	ι	ι_2
Random text	1.00	1.00
English	1.73	4.65
Russian	1.77	3.64
Italian	1.93	5.47
Spanish	1.94	6.15
Portuguese	1.94	5.67
French	2.02	6.28
German	2.04	7.47

Note: The index might vary widely from this estimate.

In practice the actual polygraphic I. C.'s will usually run higher than their theoretical values, and a repeated word or two in short texts will make them sky rocket. As typical examples, we have taken the plain text of four problems in the Navy elementary and secondary Crypt courses and computed various I. C.'s (the monographic, digraphic, trigraphic, tetragraphic and pentagraphic Indices of Coincidence).

Text	monographic	digraphic	trigraphic	tetra	penta
Expected random	1.00	1.00	1.00	1.00	1.00
Expected plain	1.75	4.65	27.89	?	?
Problem No. 1	1.80	5.23	29.11	427.	7240.
Problem No. 2	2.00	7.73	66.04	1062.	14900.
Problem No. 3	1.91	5.60	42.04	666.	12070.
Problem No. 4	1.74	4.90	31.70	456.	9190.

ORIGINAL

III. Theoretical Recapitulation.

The phenomena just described will be pictured again in general mathematical terms. Imagine text in a language with c letters. Here it may be that c = 10 for digits, or c = 24 for Greek, or c = 26 for English, or c = 50 for Japanese kana.

Suppose we have a language for which we know the proportions of the letters are $p_1, p_2, ---, p_c$.

$$p_1 + p_2 + --- + p_c = \sum_1^c p_i = 1. \tag{1}$$

Suppose further that we have two pieces of text from this language and line them up one above the other, and then count coincident letters. What is the expected number?

At a particular place the probability of a coincidence involving the i th letter is p_i^2. Therefore, the c cases being mutually exclusive, the probability of an incidence is

$$p_1^2 + p_2^2 + --- + p_c^2 = \sum_1^c p_i^2. \tag{2}$$

If the length of overlap is N, then the expected number of incidences is

$$N \sum_1^c p_i^2$$

If the text is such that $p_i = p_j = 1/c$, for all values of i and j we will refer to it as "flat", or "random". The probability of an incidence in flat text is $\sum_1^c 1/c^2 = 1/c$, and the expected number is $\frac{N}{c}$.

The ratio of the number g found in a comparison to that expected is called the "index of coincidence",

$$\iota = g \Big/ N/c = cg/N. \tag{3}$$

The expected value γ of the I. C. for our language is given by taking the expected value of g, $E(g) = N \sum_1^c p_i^2$, over the expected value for flat text or

$$\gamma = \frac{N}{N/c} \sum_1^c p_i^2 = c \sum_1^c p_i^2 \tag{4}$$

Notice that the expected value of the I.C. for flat text is 1, since $p_i = \frac{1}{c}$ is constant. This is the smallest value that γ can have. The other extreme would be for one letter to occupy every position, that is, $p_1 = 1$ and $p_i = 0$ for $i \neq 1$. Then

$$\gamma = c. \tag{5}$$

Thus we have $1 \leq \gamma \leq c$. (6)

IV. Examples of Use.

(A) TO DETERMINE WHETHER TWO MESSAGES ARE IN THE SAME KEY.

During U. S. Fleet Problem V (1925) the Battle Fleet used a cipher of their own design.

A total of 13 messages in this cipher were submitted to the Code and Signal Section for attack. Although a different indicator was used in each case, it was suspected that some of the messages might be in the same key. Two messages in one key (example No. 1) and two more in another key (example No. 2) were discovered. (The messages were eventually solved).

Each message was "lined up" with each other message and the coincidences were noted. (See examples No. 1 and No. 2).

Example No. 1

```
K T X V H J G P Z J W B J M F S U G P N S V S O P N F D N G
R O A A O R G P Z E Z G J F R Z P S O I U I Q M M F D H O F

J H U Y L I M A L S B N B J X W M P W F W V C U C D F G R L
M N R J O G O S I C Y U G U D I M D C K W Z P R P J L E R R

V G P U B X P M W C O B G X R J S P V P W C F W P G J V Q B
K L A G P A D X Y Y K H H K C I U Q P Y U O P J J F R B G X

Y F B D S L J O C N V V S L J O D S O O L P R O C G S P U A
Z B N O P O J N Y Z V T Z L S K R A J O P F Y F R X N D G E

C D B O C V D K Q B S P E L T R N V I U
G Q Q M N L Q V V A G P T Y C G C P N X J Q U E R D Q W W Q

Q Q U I I V H B K Q
```

Coincident letters are underscored. 12 coincidences occur in 140 pairs of letters.

Simple monographic coincidence.

Expected
Coincidences $\dfrac{N}{c} = \dfrac{140}{26} = 5.4$

Where N = number of letters examined.
c = number of distinct letters = 26.

$$IC = \dfrac{12.0}{5.4} = 2.2 \quad \text{(Messages are in same key)}$$

There is one repeated trigraph, GPZ, in the messages under examination. This coincidence indicates that the keys correspond at that point, but does not necessarily indicate that the keys correspond throughout the message. To verify coincidence of the keys throughout the two messages, we must have our coincidences spread through the messages in question. (As they were in the above example).

Likewise, digraphic and trigraphic coincidences may be evaluated to an index of coincidence. For example, in the above messages, 2 coincident digraphs were found (GP and PZ) (also one coincident trigraph). In this message there were 139 digraphs and 138 trigraphs in alignment with possibilities of coincidence.

$$\dfrac{N}{676} = \dfrac{139}{676} = .2$$

digraphs were to be expected from chance. Two were found, giving an IC $= \dfrac{2}{.206} = 9.7$.

This value, far above the normal 4.65 index of coincidence, does not necessarily indicate the messages are in the same key because of the smallness of the sample. The extremely high I.C., 9.70, may be due to the small amount of text involved in this example. As the amount of text decreases, the variation of the I. C. from the expected will become more pronounced, until at times it is possible that small amounts of text may give entirely false indications. This effect will be discussed more fully under "standard deviation"

Example No. 2

```
A Z E P U U Y C N O Z E S F J X C T A T M J C G G ! F K U B
B C A E Z Q Q V U Q O O E J W W D T Q Q S P F W C T O H P Z

P E K D A P N U T J D D U W Q Q I T N P E X T G H T K D C L
J S D N D U J K L U Z J C S Q H I O Z H U K E G X D E P W T

Z R P W A M M T I Q J E P K F D C O V P D U C H Z W X M G E
P R F R X P I Q V A F Q R P F E A Q P Q E W O Y E G X R O Y

Q V H I T A F F Z R Y E G O A Z B Z B G D W B J A U B E E P
Y P G A V X L A X Q E O L J O U B H B S F W J W D D J P S S

N M K O C Z D I X B Y A L V S P G P X F N U E F X N W D F L
D T E P P D Z G T J O C V H T P M R P H T Y C Q X L L V R N

A K N A V Q A X P O P R P P R P P Q P U D B L M N J Q X U E
Q F Y A X G O L U P Q F D R W D L Z W I T B D I I P Y Y V G

Q A W S Q J N G P E O A M D N Z A A P F A Z Y O T N Q W V X
U M N G C F J F L Q R M E D F O Z N S P E C D S L I Z Q Y A

I I D T W W C C Y B X O Y U O S Q D N O B A S H H C T D D U
H N I X Y A O J B K - - - - - - - - - - - - - - - - - - - -
```

There are 14 coincidences in 220 pairs of letters.

$$\frac{N}{c} = \frac{220}{26} = 8.46 \text{ coincidences expected.} \qquad IC = \frac{14}{8.46} = 1.66 \text{ (almost normal for English).}$$

These two messages *probably* are in the same key (and actually proved to be). Note that there are no repeated digraphs or trigraphs. Note also that coincidences are well spread out.

(B) TO DETERMINE WHERE TWO MESSAGES OVERLAP.

Two messages may be in depth but not at the beginnings. To place them relative to one another is the first problem prior to reading them, and this can be done by means of the I. C. if the overlap is sufficiently long. To place them the following or its equivalent should be done.

Copy each message on a single line on a separate page of paper, omitting all spaces between groups and taking care to space the letters uniformly. Then place one page upon the other so that letters of one message fall above those of the other. Note the number of coincidences and the total overlap. Then shift one message to the right and count again.

The highest index observed is the best candidate for depth. Since we have examined a number of indices some of them may be high by chance, especially for small overlaps. The interpretation of the results of such a sliding operation requires sophistication beyond the scope of this pamphlet, and will not be discussed. The simplest rule of thumb for dealing with it is to compare the highest index with the second highest. If they are close they are probably both high by chance, since only one at most can be casual; if they are disparate then the highest has a better chance of representing a depth. The digraphic and trigraphic coincidences may help decide the value of a line-up.

The process just described is a basic one, and variations of it will always be useful to the cryptanalyst.

V. The Roughness of a Single Sample.

We have introduced the comparison I. C. as a measure of the match between two pieces of text. We can extend this idea now to a measure of the roughness of a single sample. Suppose we have a piece of text which we duplicate on two slips of paper and then place them one under the other for the purpose of counting coincidences. There will be one position of total coincidence, which we will rule out. If we compute the I. C. for all other positions, we will have what we call the "index of coincidence of a single sample".

If there are M letters in our sample, we will have looked in $N = \dfrac{M(M-1)}{2}$ distinct places. (8)

If the text were drawn from a flat universe we would expect $\dfrac{N}{c} = \dfrac{M(M-1)}{2c}$ coincidences. That is, at $\dfrac{1}{c}$ of the N places there will be coincidences. (9)

If the text is not flat but proportions $p_1, p_2, \ldots, p_o$ of letters, then there are $f_i = p_i M$ occurrences of the i th letter. In the course of our counting we will compare every letter with every other, so that the i th letter will give rise to $\dfrac{f_i(f_i-1)}{2}$ coincidences, or (10)

$$\sum_{1}^{c} 1/2 \, f_i(f_i-1) \text{ in all.} \tag{11}$$

Comparing this with the expected in flat text we get the I. C.

$$\delta = \frac{\displaystyle\sum_{1}^{c} 1/2 \, f_i(f_i-1)}{\dfrac{1}{2c} M(M=1)}, \text{ or} \tag{12}$$

$$\boxed{\delta = \frac{c\displaystyle\sum_{1}^{c} f_i(f_i-1)}{M(M-1)}} \tag{13}$$

In theoretical context (12) is more useful than (13), but (13) is a little simpler for computational purposes.

Notice that this formula is different from (4). This is because of the omission of the perfect hit. If M is large enough then f_i-1 can be replaced by $f_i = p_i M$ and M−1 by M, so that

$$\delta = \frac{c\displaystyle\sum_{1}^{c} f_i^2}{M^2} = c\sum_{1}^{c} p_i^2 = \gamma \tag{14}$$

We see that

$$\delta\frac{M-1}{M} = \gamma - \frac{c}{M} \tag{15}$$

or $\boxed{\delta(M-1) = \gamma M - c}$, giving

$$\delta = \frac{\gamma M - c}{M-1} \text{ or } \gamma = \frac{\delta(M-1)+c}{M} \tag{16}$$

From (12) the expected value of δ is $E(\delta) = E\left(\dfrac{\displaystyle\sum_{1}^{c} f_i(f_i-1).}{\dfrac{1}{2c} M(M-1)}\right)$

ORIGINAL

$$=\frac{E(\Sigma f_i(f_i-1))}{\frac{1}{2c}M(M-1)}=\frac{\frac{1}{2c}M(M-1)}{\frac{1}{2c}M(M-1)}=1.$$ From this (16) gives $\quad E(\gamma)=E(\delta)\frac{M-1}{M}+\frac{c}{M}=1+\frac{c-1}{M}$

The error in using γ (usually more convenient) in place of δ is

$$\boxed{\gamma-\delta=\frac{c-\gamma}{M-1}=\frac{c-\delta}{M}.}\qquad(17)$$

This error is always positive, that is, γ is an over-estimate of δ.
The error is smaller for larger values of γ, or larger values of M.

Notice that γ is a measure of the shape of the distribution only, and is independent of the sample size, as

$$\gamma=\frac{c\Sigma f_i^2}{M^2}=\frac{c\Sigma p_i^2 M^2}{M^2}=c\Sigma p_i^2,\qquad(18)$$

since $f_i=p_i M$.

But δ does depend on the sample size M, which is a desirable characteristic, since random roughness is usually present in small samples. For smaller samples

$$\delta=\gamma-\frac{c-\gamma}{M-1}\qquad(19)$$

is seen to be smaller, thus automatically compensating to some degree for small sample errors.

We will usually measure the roughness of single samples by δ, using γ as an asymptotic approximation.

VI. Examination of Cipher Alphabets and Cipher Texts and Coherence.

The indices of coincidences discussed in the previous paragraphs may be used in analyzing the internal structure of a cipher alphabet. For example, a message of 173 letters has a frequency table as given below:

A	B	C	D	E	F	G	H	I	J	K	L	M	N	O	P	Q	R	S	T	U	V	W	X	Y	Z
6	3	0	14	2	2	10	22	6	4	8	13	1	0	14	10	0	13	2	13	0	7	19	1	2	1

We count the number of times a letter occurs with the same frequency, thus:

Tally	Number of tallies	$f(f-1)$	$nf(f-1)$
f	n	2	2
0	4	0	0
1	3	0	0
2	4	1	4
3	1	3	3
4	1	6	6
6	2	15	30
7	1	21	21
8	1	28	28
10	2	45	90
13	3	78	234
14	2	91	182
19	1	171	171
22	1	231	231
			1000

9

We obtain the I.C. by formula (13):

$$\delta = \frac{c\Sigma f_i(f_i-1)}{M(M-1)}$$

Substituting.

$$\delta = \frac{1000 \times 52}{173 \times 172} = 1.75$$

The index of coincidence indicates that a monoalphabetic substitution was employed.

As a second example to show the results obtained from small texts, we calculate as follows from a frequency count of 36 letters assumed to be monoalphabetic.

A	3	N	2
B		O	1
C	5	P	
D		Q	
E		R	1
F	3	S	3
G	1	T	1
H	1	U	2
I	1	V	
J		W	1
K		X	4
L	3	Y	4
M		Z	

Tally f	n	$\frac{f(f-1)}{2}$	$n\frac{f(f-1)}{1}$
0	10		
1	7	0	0
2	2	1	2
3	4	3	12
4	2	6	12
5	1	10	10
			36

$$\delta = \frac{36 \times 26 \times 2}{36 \times 35} = 1.49.$$

The alphabet in question was actually a monoalphabetic substitution With a small amount of text, the simple index is somewhat indeterminate. *It is again emphasized that sufficient text must be used to give positive indications.*

As another elementary example of the application of the index of coincidence to the internal examination of a cipher text, we have a 5-letter repetition at an interval of 85. Is the cipher a polyalphabetic cipher of 5 or 17 alphabets? By means of internal examination with the index of coincidence we can decide between these alternatives.

Make a frequency count of the cipher alphabets assuming 5 and then 17 alphabets. Calculate the index of coincidence in each case for one or more pairs of alphabets. The indices of higher value will indicate which assumption is correct. If neither assumption shows positive results (an index around 1.7) we may have a cipher of more complex nature.

Another elementary application is as follows. We have a cipher message which has been intercepted. The I. C. is computed and found to be $\delta = 1.79$. This is so rough as to resemble plain text. A simple substitution has the property of leaving δ unchanged, and so has a transposition. Polyalphabetic substitutions lower the I. C.. So we are reduced to three hypotheses, that our sample is either transposed plain text, a simple substitution, or both substitution and transposition.

The digraphic I. C. is computed, $\delta_2 = 4.85$. Its expected value is $\delta_2 = 3.05$ in view of the known monographic roughness. Since a transposition destroys coherence the evidence is that no transposition is involved. Polygraphic Indices of coincidence are preserved by a simple substitution.

VII. The Standard Deviation.

We have already several times referred to the fact that these statistics are useful only if the sample is large enough. To get an idea as to whether this is the case or not we measure our results in terms of a standard deviation, "sigma." One standard deviation is roughly one half the width of a band which when placed about the average will include two-thirds of the data. It is a measure of the dispersion. If sigma is large the data is spread out wide, and if it is small the numbers are close together. In a binomial distribution the standard deviation is $\delta = \sqrt{Npq}$ where N is the number of observations and p and q are the probabilities of successs and failure.

To estimate the significance of δ, we refer to (12), where the denominator is the expected number of incidences in flat text, and the numerator is the number found. The standard deviation

of δ is $\sigma(\delta) = \sqrt{\dfrac{2(c-1)}{M(M-1)}}$, see Appendix III. That is, in the first $\hspace{2cm}$ (20)

example of the previous section $\delta = 1.75$, and $\sigma(\delta) = \sqrt{\dfrac{2 \times 25}{173 \times 172}} = .04$. Thus δ is $\dfrac{.75}{.04} = 19$ standard deviations above the value expected from a flat universe. In the second example of the

previous section, $\delta = 1.49$ and $\sigma(\delta) = \sqrt{\dfrac{2(26-1)}{36 \times 35}} = \dfrac{5}{126} = .2$.

Thus δ is $\dfrac{.49}{.2}$ above the expected value of 1, or $2\frac{1}{2}$ standard deviations. The significance to be

attached to this will be discussed later.

If S is the "sigmage" or the deviation from expected in terms of σ we have

$$S = \frac{\delta - 1}{\sqrt{\dfrac{2(c-1)}{M(M-1)}}} = (\delta - 1)\sqrt{\frac{M(M-1)}{2(c-1)}} \hspace{2cm} (21)$$

Using the γ I.C. we get

$$S = \frac{\gamma - 1}{\sqrt{\dfrac{2(c-1)\ (M-1)}{M^3}}} = \frac{\gamma - 1}{\sqrt{2(c-1)}}\sqrt{\frac{M^2}{M-1}}, \hspace{2cm} (22)$$

using the results of Appendix III.

In either case approximately

$$S = \frac{\gamma - 1}{\sqrt{2(c-1)}}M \quad \text{or} \quad S = \frac{\delta - 1}{\sqrt{2(c-1)}}M, \hspace{2cm} (23)$$

with an error introduced by this approximation of less than 1% for $M > 51$.

Notice that the sigmage is approximately a linear function of the sample size M, and also linear with the "bulge" $\delta - 1$. The denominator is relatively unimportant to the estimation of S except in shifting from code to cipher, when c can change from 500,000 to as small as 10.

The bulge $\beta = \delta - 1$ is a quantity which will recur frequently.

Formula (21) does not apply to the comparison I.C. For that we have the expected number N/c and g found.

Then $\sigma^2 = N/c(1-1/c)$ and the sigmage is

$$S = \frac{g - N/c}{\sqrt{N/c(1-1/c)}} = \frac{gc/N-1}{\sqrt{\frac{c-1}{N}}} = \frac{\iota-1}{\sqrt{c-1}}\sqrt{N}. \tag{24}$$

In this case the sigmage is linear with the bulge $\iota - 1$, but varies only as the square root of the sample size. It is important to use formulas (21) and (24) in the right contexts, and not confuse them.

The significance of $S(\delta)$ is given in the table of Appendix VI, which lists the probability of getting $S(\delta)$ or a larger result from chance.

In Appendix VI it is shown that the probability of δ attaining a limit, Prob $(\delta \geq \delta_0)$, is the same as the probability of the sigmage S attaining another related limit, Prob $(S \geq S_0)$. The advantage of using sigmage is that the probability is independent of the sample size, a great convenience in tabulating. The tables of Appendix VI enable one to estimate the significance of a sigmage as a probability.

If a probability Prob $(S \geq S_0)$ is not in the table of Appendix VI then the entry $P\left(\frac{c-1}{2}, \frac{b}{2}\right)$

is a good approximation, $b = S_0\sqrt{2(c-1)} + c - 1$, where $P(x,a)$ is the Poisson cumulative function, tabulated in the Cryptanalyst's Manual, Section 5-1, Table II, published by the National Security Agency. If the probability is too small even for the Poisson tables then it is closely approximated

by Prob $(S \leq k) \doteq \frac{a^k e^{-a}}{k!}$ where $a = \frac{N(N-1)}{2c}$.

For the comparison I.C. a different table must be used. Since $\iota = \frac{g}{N/c}$ and the distribution of g is binomial, then Prob $(g \geq k)$ is given by $P(k, \frac{N}{c})$ the Poisson distribution, and the approximation is good if c is large. From this Prob $(\iota \geq k) \doteq P(k\frac{N}{c}, \frac{N}{c})$. Entries too small to be

in the table are closely approximated by $\frac{a^x e^{-a}}{x!}$, where $a = \frac{N}{c}$ and $x = k\frac{N}{c}$.

Example: A cipher message is suspected of being in depth with itself at interval 676. It is 1352 letters in length, giving an overlap of 676. Thus there are 26 coincidences expected from chance between the first and second halves. There are 50 observed. What is the significance of this? The Poisson table shows that this many or more will occur .000013, or only about once in a hundred thousand such experiments by chance.

VIII. The Cross I. C.

Suppose we have two stretches of text of which the distributions are given by $p_1, p_2, ---$ p_c and $q_1, q_2, ---, q_c$,

$$\sum_1^c p_i = 1, \qquad \sum_1^c q_i = 1.$$

If these texts are placed one above the other the probability of an incidence at any one position is

$$\sum_{i=1}^{c} p_i q_i \qquad (25)$$

and the expected comparison I.C. is

$$\xi = c\Sigma p_i q_i.$$

We can show that the expected value of ξ is 1.
If one of the samples of text is flat, say $q_i = 1/c$, then

$$\xi = 1, \qquad (26)$$

for

$$\xi = c\Sigma p_i q_i = c/c\Sigma p_i = 1 \times 1 = 1.$$

If both samples are rough, then ξ fluctuates widely as the q's are permuted. The question arises, how wide is the distribution of ξ.

A standard measure is the "variance"

$$\sigma^2 = E(\xi^2) - [E(\xi)]^2. \qquad (27)$$

From Appendix II we conclude

$$\boxed{\sigma^2 = \frac{(P-1)(Q-1)}{c-1}} \qquad (33)$$

where $P = c\Sigma p_i^2$ and $Q = c\Sigma q_i^2$ are the I.C.'s of the two texts.

This says that the square of a standard deviation σ is the product of the bulges over $c-1$.

$$S = \frac{\xi - 1}{\frac{\sqrt{(P-1)(Q-1)}}{c-1}} = (\xi - 1)\sqrt{\frac{c-1}{(P-1)(Q-1)}}$$

is a measure of the significance which can be judged from the table of Appendix VI.

The function ξ can be used as a measure of correlation between two distributions.

IX. The Coincidence Test Used to Align Secondary Alphabets into a Primary Alphabet.

We give here a special application of the I. C. statistic. An actual problem from an elementary course is used. Special frequency distribution tables were made of the sample lined up into 26 columns, i. e., lines of 26 letters each.

This problem happens to be enciphered by means of a Vigenère table, the columns being used in succession. Consequently if the cipher text is lined up 26 wide each column is enciphered by a monoalphabetic substitution. Each alphabet is a slide on that in the next column. If we knew the plain and cipher sequences the text could be decrypted. The problem is to recover these sequences. Since the sequence is not alphabetical, adjacent frequency counts as given in table C appear unrelated. But if we look at the rows they must be related by being slides of each other. If we can establish these slides we will have the cipher sequence.

By use of this special table, table "C", we can build up the cipher component used by matching these frequency distributions. In selecting distributions to match we want to obtain rows which have:

(a) A maximum total number of letters involved (as the distribution will then be more reliable).

(b) A distribution with a normal count (i. e., similar to English).

Table "C" -- Frequency Table of the Cryptogram

Column → Cipher ↓	1	26	25	24	23	22	21	20	19	18	17	16	15	14	13	12	11	10	9	8	7	6	5	4	3	2	Total Letters
A	1	3		3				2		5		3	2							1		2		1	2		25
B		1	3	1		4	4	1				2	5		5		2	3	1			1			1	2	36
C		2		1	1						1		3	2			1	1			3			1	2		18
D				1		1			2	1	1		1		7				4		3			1			22
E				1	2	2			2		3			1		1	1	1				1	4	5	1		25
F				1					1	1	2					1	1		2		1		1	2		1	14
G	1	1			1	5		1	1	2	1		1		2					1	1	1		2	3	2	26
H	3		2		1	1						2		1		2			1		1	1	1			1	17
I		1			2			1			1	1	1	1	1	1	2	1			3					4	18
J			3	1	3		3						1			2		1	4		1			1	2		22
K	4	1			2				1	3			1	3	1	2	2		2			3		2		2	27
L			1				4				3	2			3			1			3			1	1	1	20
M	1		1	3		1	1	1	2		3		5			1	1		1	1			1	1	1	1	22
N		1						3	3				4	3	1		1	2		2		2	2				24
O	3		2	1				1	1				2			2	1	1			1					1	16
P				3	3				1			1				1			4	4				1			17
Q				1			1					5	1				1	1	2			2			2	2	16
R		1	1	2		1			2	4	1	1		2		1		3	1		1		1			2	24
S	2		3		1	2					4			2		1				2		1	3				21
T		2	1		1								4	3	1		3			5			1	3		2	26
U	1			1	1	4	1	3	1		2			2		1		2				2					19
V	4	2			1				1	1		1		1	1	1		3	2			3	2		3	1	27
W		4	1	1		1	2				1						3	3		1	3	2		1			13
X	1				1		2			1		1		1			1		4	1		1	2	1			17
Y		1				1	2	3	1	1			2			1					3	1	2		1		19
Z	1	1	2			1				2			1	2		1		1			1		1				15

Table "D" -- Sliding Strips

: Plain	: 1	2	3	4	5	6	7	8	9	1Ø	11	12	13	14	15	16	17	18	19	2Ø	21	22	23	24	25	26:	"B" Master Distribution :
: Cipher	: B																									:	:
: Freq.	:	1	3	1		4	4	1					2	5		5		2	3	1			1		1	2:	1 3 1 4 4 1 2 5 :

| | : | | 2 | 1 | | 1 | | | | | | | | 4 | 3 | 1 | | 3 | | | 5 | | | 1 | 3 | | 2: | "T" set at 2 on the "B" : |
| | : T | | | | | | | | | | | | | | | | | | | | | | | | | | | Master Distribution. |

| | :1 | 3 | | 3 | | | | 2 | | 5 | | 3 | 2 | | | | | 1 | | 2 | | 1 | 2 | | | : | |
| | :A | | | | | | | | | | | | | | | | | | | | | | | | | : | |

| | : | 1 | | | | | | 3 | 3 | | | 4 | 3 | 1 | | | 1 | 2 | | 2 | | 2 | 2 | | | : | |
| | : N | | | | | | | | | | | | | | | | | | | | | | | | | : | |

: Plain	: 1	2	3	4	5	6	7	8	9	1Ø	11	12	13	14	15	16	17	18	19	2Ø	21	22	23	24	25	26:	T-1- -- N-5- Master :
: Cipher	: T				N																					:	Distribution. :
: Freq.	:	4	3		1	1						7	6	1			7	3	1	5			2	5		4:	4 3 1 1 7 6 1 :

| | : | | | | | | | | | | | 1 | 3 | 1 | | 4 | 4 | 1 | | | 2 | 5 | | 5 | 2 3 1 | 1 1 2 : | |
| | :B | | | | | | | | | | | | | | | | | | | | | | | | | | |

| | : | | | | | | | | | | | | 1 | 3 | | 5 | | | 2 | | 5 | 3 2 | | 1 2 1 : | | |
| | :A | | | | | | | | | | | | | | | | | | | | | | | | | |

16

Table "E" -- Table of Total Coincidences

B = Master Distribution

```
                                                                                    Chance
                                                                                    Coinci-
Plain -1  2  3  4  5  6  7  8  9 10 11 12 13 14 15 16 17 18 19 20 21 22 23 24 25 26  dences
Cipher-B
  T  -X 43 49 -- 39 -- -- -- 59 -- -- -- 53 -- -- 41 40 37 -- 60 -- -- -- -- 64 -- -- -- -- 39   36
  A  -X -- -- 38 66 -- 59 -- -- -- -- -- 42 -- -- -- -- -- -- -- 50 -- 42 -- -- --   35
  N  -X -- -- 53 40 -- -- -- -- -- -- -- -- -- -- -- -- -- 43 39 63 -- -- -- -- --   33
```

> NOTE: The numbers 43, 49, etc., represent the successive numbers
> of "coincidences", i.e., the sums of products of
> frequencies at successive points of coincidence.

T = Master Distribution

```
Plain -1  2  3  4  5  6  7  8  9 10 11 12 13 14 15 16 17 18 19 20 21 22 23 24 25 26
Cipher-T
  A  -X -- 32 -- -- -- -- 28 29 -- 42 -- -- -- 31 -- 51 -- 43 -- -- -- -- -- -- --   25
  N  -X -- -- 28 50 -- 28 26 -- -- -- 34 -- -- -- 34 -- -- -- 31 -- -- -- -- -- 32 34   24
```

A = Master Distribution

```
Plain -1  2  3  4  5  6  7  8  9 10 11 12 13 14 15 16 17 18 19 20 21 22 23 24 25 26
Cipher-A
  N  -X -- 26 -- -- -- -- -- -- -- -- 28 26 -- 43 -- 34 27 -- -- -- -- 27 29 -- 27   23
```

T - 1 -- N - 5 = Master Distribution

```
                N
Plain -1  2  3  4  5  6  7  8  9 10 11 12 13 14 15 16 17 18 19 20 21 22 23 24 25 26
Cipher-T        N
  B  -X -- -- -- X -- 100 - -- -- 123 - 80 78 74 -- -- -- -- -- 82 -- 75 73 89 96   69
  A  -X -- -- -- -- -- -- -- 57 56 -- 61 -- -- 65 -- 94 -- 65 -- -- -- -- -- -- --   48
```

17

Table "T" -- Table of Coincidences

Master Distribution T-1 N-5 B-11 A-17

Plain →	1	2	3	4	5	6	7	8	9	10	11	12	13	14	15	16	17	18	19	20	21	22	23	24	25	26	Chance Coincidences
Cipher ↓	T/T	V	I	D	N/N	Y	U	F	P	M	B/B	K	H	Q	Z	E	A/A	L	G	X	R	J	W	S	C	O	
K	X	149	-	-	X	-	-	-	-	-	X	175	-	-	-	-	X	-	-	-	-	-	-	-	-	156	120
V	X	181	-	-	X	-	-	-	-	-	X	X	-	-	-	-	X	-	-	-	-	143	-	-	-	158	120
D	X	X	-	193	X	-	-	165	-	-	X	X	-	-	-	-	X	-	-	-	-	143	-	-	-	-	94
E	X	X	135	-	X	-	-	-	-	-	X	X	-	-	-	190	X	-	-	-	-	148	-	-	-	-	102
W	X	X	-	-	X	-	-	-	129	-	X	X	-	-	-	X	X	-	-	-	-	-	200	-	-	-	102
G	X	X	-	-	X	-	-	-	-	-	X	X	-	143	X	X	-	-	193	131	-	X	-	-	-	-	107
R	X	X	-	-	X	-	-	-	133	-	X	X	-	-	-	-	X	X	-	X	-	158	-	X	-	-	102
M	X	X	133	-	X	-	-	-	-	155	X	X	-	144	-	X	X	-	X	-	X	-	X	-	-	-	94
J	X	X	-	-	X	-	-	-	-	-	X	X	-	-	-	-	X	X	-	X	-	170	X	-	-	-	90
L	X	X	-	-	X	144	-	-	-	-	X	X	-	-	-	-	X	154	X	-	X	X	X	-	-	-	90
S	X	X	-	-	X	-	-	110	-	-	X	X	-	-	109	X	-	X	-	X	-	X	X	159	-	-	90
C	X	X	117	-	X	-	-	-	-	-	X	X	-	-	-	-	X	X	-	X	-	X	X	X	172	-	81
U	X	X	-	-	X	119	90	-	-	-	X	X	-	-	-	-	X	X	-	X	-	X	X	X	X	-	81
Y	X	X	-	-	X	153	-	93	-	96	X	X	-	-	-	-	X	X	-	X	-	X	X	X	X	X	81
I	X	X	121	-	X	X	X	94	-	-	X	X	109	-	-	-	X	X	X	X	-	X	X	X	X	X	77
H	X	X	X	-	X	X	X	-	-	-	X	X	119	-	86	X	X	X	X	-	X	X	X	X	X	90	73
P	X	X	X	-	X	X	X	-	142	-	X	X	X	-	-	X	X	X	X	116	X	X	X	X	X	-	73
X	X	X	X	-	X	X	X	110	X	-	X	X	X	-	-	X	X	X	X	139	X	X	X	X	X	-	73
O	X	X	X	-	X	X	X	-	X	-	X	-	X	X	-	-	X	X	X	X	X	X	X	X	X	117	68
Q	X	X	X	-	X	X	X	-	X	81	-	X	-	108	X	-	X	X	X	X	X	X	X	X	X	X	68
Z	X	X	X	-	X	X	X	-	X	X	X	X	-	X	113	X	X	X	X	X	X	X	X	X	X	X	64
F	X	X	X	72	X	X	X	87	X	X	X	X	X	X	X	X	X	X	X	X	X	X	X	X	X	X	60

(c) A distribution without any one letter of abnormal frequency (as this gives too much weight to one letter).

When frequency distributions of two letters are properly matched, high should pair with high, low with low, blank with blank, etc. The mathematical value of each relative position is found as follows:

(a) With the two frequency distributions in question written on paper strips and slid one against the other, for any one position we multiply the frequencies in alignment, and then add the products of all these multiplications. (see table "D").

(b) Cross-multiply the total count of the first distribution by the count of the second. This is the total number of possible pairs of letters. Chance would produce one coincidence in twenty-six. Therefore, divide this product by twenty-six, which gives the number of expected chance coincidences.

(c) Divide the number of the actual coincidences by the expected number of chance coincidences. The resulting number is the *Index of Coincidence*.

To prove correct alignment:

(a) The index for the given relative position of two distributions must be higher than for all other positions, with no close second.

(b) The index should be 1.50 or higher (preferably 1.73 or higher).

(c) There must be only one acceptable alignment.

Indeterminate results will be encountered in some cases, particularly with insufficient text.

Table "E" gives the coincidences at various positions of one strip slid against another.

From table "C", it is seen that certain distributions have the following properties (referring to our three desired properties):

Row B (cipher) has a total of 36 letters, with 14 different letters involved. Its highest frequency is 5. Good. Approaches normality. Maximum text.

V (cipher) has a total of 27 letters with 15 different letters involved. Its highest frequency is 4. Not good—too flat.

K (cipher) has a total of 27 letters with 13 different letters involved. Its highest frequency is 5. Not good—too flat.

G (cipher) has a total of 25 letters with 15 different letters involved. Its highest frequency is 5. Not good—too flat.

D (cipher) has a total of 22 letters with only 10 different letters involved, but its highest frequency is 7. Not good—too peaked.

T (cipher) has a total of 26 letters with 11 different letters involved. Its highest frequency is 5. Good. Approaches normality.

A (cipher) has a total of 25 letters with 11 different letters involved. Its highest frequency is 5. Good. Approaches normality.

N (cipher) has a total of 24 letters with 11 different letters involved. Its highest frequency is 4. Good. Approaches normality.

B, T, A and N are the best rows. Match T, A, and N against B, then match A and N against T, finally match N against A. One of these combinations sould give a positive index of coincidence, and thus serve as a starting point.

Building Up The Cipher Component

By utilizing the principles described in the previous sections, we can build up the cipher component. Take B (cipher) as the master distribution, since it is acceptable and contains the highest count. Copy the frequencies of B (from "C") at the bottom of a strip of paper, and repeat this sequence to the right. Over the first sequence write the numbers 1 to 26 as shown in table "D". Under No. 1 write the letters "B". The numbers represent the various unknown letters of the cipher component. Make similar master distribution strips for T and A. Next, copy the distribution of T (cipher) (from table "D") at the top of a strip of paper. Only one sequence is required for this strip, and the numbers are omitted. Indicate the space corresponding to column No. 1 (table "D") by the letter T (see table "E"). In a like manner make strips for A and N.

> *Note:* The letter on each strip is an indicator to mark column No. 1 for that letter. When strips are properly aligned, the indicators show the relative positions of these letters in the cipher component. The student is advised to prepare strips for himself and follow these processes.

First, match T against B. As no two letters can occupy the same position in the cipher component, begin by setting the T indicator at No. 2 on the B master alphabet. Count the coincidences. Next, slide T to No. 3, and count the coincidences. Continue this process to No. 26, and record the successive numbers of coincidences in tabular form (see table "F"). In many cases lack of sufficient coincidences will be obvious by inspection and the count need not be made. In this way we discover that B and T give high indices of coincidence in two different alignments (indices computed in accordance with rule in page 30).

$$\text{Index of B (1)} - \text{T (7)} \quad \frac{64}{36} = 1.77 \quad \text{(good)}$$

$$\text{Index of B (1)} - \text{T (11)} \quad \frac{60}{36} = 1.67 \quad \text{(good)}$$

All other alignments give such low indices that they can be at once eliminated. The above two indices, however, are both high enough to be significant, and as the second is so close to the first, it cannot be disregarded.

There can be only one acceptable point of coincidence; therefore, it is necessary to match A against B, and N against B, to see if more conclusive results can be attained.

$$\text{Index of B (1)} - \text{A (5)} \quad \frac{66}{36} = 1.89 \quad \text{(excellent)}$$

$$\text{Index of B (1)} - \text{A (7)} \quad \frac{59}{35} = 1.69 \quad \text{(good)}$$

(Other alignments are eliminated)

$$\text{Index of B (1)} - \text{N (21)} \quad \frac{63}{33} = 1.91 \quad \text{(excellent)}$$

$$\text{Index of B (1)} - \text{N (6)} \quad \frac{53}{33} = 1.60 \quad \text{(fair)}$$

(Other alignments are eliminated)

Since there is no outstanding coincidence with "B" as the "master alphabet", try "T" and "A" as the "master alphabet":

$$\text{Index of T (1)} - \text{A (17)} \quad \frac{51}{25} = 2.04 \quad \text{(excellent)}$$

$$\text{Index of T (1)} - \text{A (19)} \quad \frac{43}{25} = 1.72 \quad \text{(good)}$$

Index of T (1) − A (11) $\frac{42}{25} = 1.68$ (good)

Index of T (1) − N (5) $\frac{50}{24} = 2.08$ (excellent)

Index of T (1) − N (12) $\frac{34}{24} = 1.42$ (poor)
         (16)
         (26)

Index of A (1) − N (15) $\frac{43}{23} = 1.87$ (good)

Index of A (1) − N (17) $\frac{34}{23} = 1.48$ (poor)

The most certain combination is T (1) − N (5), and there is no doubt as to its correctness. This located "N" relative to "T" in the cipher component, and allows us to consolidate their frequencies.

For a new master distribution add the frequencies of T (at space No. 1) to those of N (at space No. 5) (see table "E"). Match "B" and "A" against this new master distribution:

Index of T (1) & N (5) − B (11) $\frac{123}{69} = 1.81$ (good)

Index of T (1) & N (5) − B (7) $\frac{100}{69} = 1.45$ (poor)

Index of T (1) & N (5) − B (26) $\frac{76}{69} = 1.40$ (poor)

Index of T (1) & N (5) − A (17) $\frac{94}{48} = 1.96$ (excellent)

Index of T (1) & N (5) − A (15) $\frac{65}{48} = 1.35$ (very poor)

Index of T (1) & N (5) − A (19) $\frac{65}{48} = 1.35$ (very poor)

"B" and "A" can now be consolidated with "T" and "N" for the final "master distribution" as follows:

Plain −	1	2	3	4	5	6	7	8	9	10	11	12	13
Cipher −	T				N								
T & N		4	3		1	1						7	6
B		2	3	1			1		1	2		1	3
A		3	2							1		2	

Plain −	14	15	16	17	18	19	20	21	22	23	24	25	26
Cipher −													
T & N	1			7	3	1	5			2	5		4
B	1		4	4	1					2	5		5
A	1	2		1	3		3				2		5

This locates "B" and "A" relative to "T" and "N" in the cipher component, in addition to giving the combined frequencies of all four letters.

FINAL MASTER DISTRIBUTION

Plain	− 1	2	3	4	5	6	7	8	9	10	11	12	13
Cipher	− T				N						B		
Comb.	−	9	8	1	1	1	1		1	3		10	9
Freq.													

Plain	− 14	15	16	17	18	19	20	21	22	23	24	25	26
Cipher	−			A									
Comb.	− 3	2	4	12	7	1	8		4	12			14
Freq.													

Analyze the preceding steps. T gave two possible alignments with B, and, as we now see, the incorrect position gave the higher index. N also gave two possible alignments with B. (B was at fault due to its erratic letter distribution). However, when T and N are combined, giving twice as many letters in the master distribution, B fitted in with only one possible alignment. adding B and A gives twice as many letters in the master distribution and this should make future results even more positive. The master distribution (of 100 letters or more) should approximate a normal frequency distribution and will give a standard to which all the other distributions can be referred. Hereafter, variations in the highest index of coincidence will be due entirely to letter distribution of the various distributions themselves.

For example:

If the highest index is 1.7 − letter distribution is normal.

If the highest index is 2.0 − high frequency letters predominate.

If the highest index is 1.4 − the intermediate and low frequency letters predominate.

Therefore, when matching the remaining letters, we can accept the *highest* index of coincidence as establishing coincidence, unless the second highest is too high.

Continue the matching process and the reconstruction of the cipher component, noting that T, N, B and A are already located and thus may be deleted at once from further test. Begin with the letters of the highest frequency, as they should give the most positive results. When a letter is placed, delete this location from further test, as two letters cannot occupy the same space in the cipher component.

Letters are added to the cipher component in the following order (see table "F"):

"Master alphabet" T (1) − N (5) − B (11) − A (17)

K (12) 1.46 (poor − but acceptable)
V (2) 1.51 (poor − but acceptable)
D (4) 2.05 (excellent)
D (8) 1.76 (good) (D − not certain)
E (16) 1.86 (excellent)
W (23) 1.96 (excellent)
G (19) 1.80 (good)

Note: With this many values a key-word (if any) sequence could be completed by inspection. In this case, the partially reconstructed cipher component gives no suggestion of a key-word sequence.

ORIGINAL

R (21) 1.55 (fair but acceptable)
M (10) 1.65 (good)
M (14) 0.53 (M — not certain)
J (22) 1.89 (excellent)
L (18) 1.71 (good)
L (6) 1.60 (fair) (L — not certain)
S (24) 1.77 (good)
C (25) 2.12 (excellent)
U (7) 1.47 (poor but acceptable)
Y (6) 1.89 (excellent)

    Note: This throws out L (6), but leaves L (18) as correct.

I (3)   (fair)
l (13) 1.42 (poor) (I — not certain)
H (13) 1.63 (good)

    Note: This throws out I (13) and leaves I (3) as correct.

P (9) 1.95 (excellent)
X (20) 1.90 (excellent)
O (26) 1.72 (good)
Q (14) 1.59 (fair and acceptable)

    Note: This throws out M (14) and leaves M (10) as correct.

Z (15) 1.77 (good)
F (8) 1.45 (poor but acceptable)
F (4) 1.20 (very poor)
F (8) is correct and D (4) is correct

The cipher component has now been completely recovered.

    Note: The process described above has actually built up the complete squared-cipher-table of a modified Vigenère table (it remains only to recover the plain component to complete the Vigenère table). We have written down the cipher component rather than the complete square table merely to save time and effort.

X. The I. C. of the Modular Sum of Two Streams.

Consider two streams, one of I. C. $\gamma_1 = c \Sigma q_i^2$, the other of I. C. $\gamma_2 = c \Sigma r_i^2$. If these streams are added letter by letter mod c, what is the expected value of the γ I. C. of the sum, assuming independence of the two streams?

It is $\gamma = 1 + \dfrac{(\gamma_1 - 1)(\gamma_2 - 1)}{c - 1}$. If we write $\beta = \gamma - 1$,   (34)

the bulge, then $\beta = \dfrac{\beta_1 \beta_1}{c - 1}$. For proof see Appendix IV.   (35)

Example: A certain cipher system works as follows. The clerk picks a verse from the Bible. He copies this verse and succeeding verses until he has enough for his purpose. Then he copies underneath it the plain text of his message. Then using a Vigenère square he combines the two, getting cipher text. This is "modular" addition.

The cipher text will have a certain roughness. If the I. C. of his plain text is 1.7, and that of the Bible is 1.8, then the bulge of the cipher will be $\dfrac{.7 \times .8}{25} = .02$ approximately. The I. C. of the cipher text is expected to be 1.02.

 ORIGINAL

XI. The Roughness of Mixed Texts.

What happens to the I. C. when the text is made up of letters coming from two distributions? To fix our ideas, suppose that there are two streams of text available with I. C.s 1.0 and 2.0 respectively. Then a new text is made up by taking a letter from one and then a letter from the other, repeating this until a sufficient sample is obtained. What should the I. C. of the mixture be?

The answer is 1.25, which we can derive quickly this way. Suppose the frequencies of the first stream to be $q_1, q_2, --$, with $c\Sigma q_i^2 = 1$, and those of the second stream to be $s_1, s_2, --$ with $c\Sigma s_i^2 = 2$. Then the frequency p_i of a letter in the mixed sample is $p_i = \frac{1}{2}q_i + \frac{1}{2}s_i$. Then

$$\gamma = c\Sigma p_i^2 = c\Sigma(\frac{s_i + q_i}{2})^2 = \frac{c}{4}(\Sigma s_i^2 + 2\Sigma s_i q_i + \Sigma q_i^2)$$

$= \frac{1}{4} \times 1 + \frac{1}{2}\xi + \frac{1}{4} \times 2 = \frac{1}{2}\xi + \frac{3}{4}$, where ξ is the cross I.C. of the two components. The expected values of the cross I.C. is 1, as in VIII, so the expected value of γ is $\frac{1}{2} \times 1 + \frac{3}{4} = 1\frac{1}{4}$.

A similar argument (given in Appendix V) shows that if there are mixed a number k of texts with bulges β_i, each present in the proportion γ_i where $\sum_{i=1}^{k} \gamma_i = 1$, then the expected bulge of the mixture is $\gamma - 1 = \sum_{i=1}^{k} \gamma_i^2 \beta_1$. (36)

That is each contributes to the roughness according to the square of its presence. This is true only if the k distributions are unrelated.

Example: Suppose a body of traffic consisting of 25 messages from a cipher system which for a given key gives an expected I.C. of 1.04. However, the messages are actually in two different keys, 10 from one key and 15 from another. What is the expected I.C.?

$$E(\gamma) = 1 + .04(\frac{2}{5})^2 + .04(\frac{3}{5})^2$$

$$= 1 + .04(\frac{4+9}{25}) = 1 + .01\frac{52}{25} \doteq 1.02$$

XII. The Relation Between Chi-Square and the Gamma I.C.

The chi-square test is a standard statistic for comparing two distributions. It is more flexible than the I.C. and its use has been described in many places. It is also more tricky than the I.C., its very flexibility making it hard for a beginner to use intelligently.

If f_i and g_i are the frequencies of corresponding objects in two counts of the same size

$$N = \sum_{i=1}^{c} f_i = \sum_{i=1}^{c} g_i,$$

then $\chi^{02} = \sum_{i=1}^{c} \frac{(f_i - g_i)^2}{g_i}$

is the usual definition of the chi-square test. The frequency g_i may be the expected value of f_i from some universe with probabilities p_i, so that $g_i = E(f_i) = p_i N$. Then (37) becomes

$$\chi^{02} = \sum_{i=1}^{c} \frac{(f_i - p_i N)^2}{p_i N} = \frac{1}{N}\Sigma \frac{f_i^2}{p_i} - N.$$ (38)

All the predictions for the I.C. are made from the flat universe for which $p_i = 1/c$. Then (38) becomes

$$\chi^{02} = \frac{c}{N} \Sigma f_i{}^2 - N = N\gamma - N = N(\gamma - 1). \tag{39}$$

This simple relation shows that under the assumption used, that the universe is flat, the chi-square test and the I.C. are essentially the same thing. The delta I.C. has a fixed expected value, 1, which does not depend on the elusive number of degrees of freedom, and this is somewhat of an advantage. The probabilities of various scores, the "distribution", for the I.C. can be devised from that of chi-square. If the use of the chi-square test is indicated, as when the probabilities p_i of the universe are not all equal, the cryptanalyst is referred to to the paper "The Chi-square Test" by Greenwood, Lotz, and Barrett, AFSA-34, 14 March 1952.

XIII. The I.C. of a Rectangular Array.

It frequently happens that the cryptanalyst makes counts in a rectangular pattern, as for instance a set of frequency counts on a cipher using several alphabets, one column for each alphabet, one row for each letter. After the counts have been made the question arises, is this array significant? The I.C. can be applied to each column, or to each row, but the numbers thus obtained will not be independent, nor will they reflect recognizably the interdependences. A number of ways of dealing with this problem have been used, and no one method is outstanding. The cross I.C. or the chi-square between columns are sometimes used. The student is referred to "Statistics for Cryptology," AFSA 14, 1 December 1951, by H. Campaigne.

One treatment worthy of mention here is due to Dr. H. Gingerich. It is aimed only at measuring the information contained in a rectangular array, and not at extracting the information.

Suppose the count in the ith row and jth column is f_{ij}. Let t_j be the total for the jth column, $t_j = \sum_{i=1}^{n} f_{ij}$. Compute the delta I.C. of each column. To do this first compute

$$N_j = \sum_{i=1}^{n} f_{ij}(f_{ij}-1) \tag{40}$$

and $D_j = \frac{1}{c} t_j(t_j - 1)$. Then $\tag{41}$

$\delta_j = \frac{1}{2}N_j / \frac{1}{2}D_j = N_j / D_j$. Now form

$$\bar{\delta} = \frac{\sum_{j=1}^{w} N_j}{\sum_{j=1}^{w} D_j}, \text{ a sort of average of the I.C.'s. This is seen} \tag{42}$$

to have the expected value $E(\bar{\delta}) = 1$, since $E(N_j) = D_j$, and it

can be shown to have the variance $\sigma^2 = \sum_{j=1}^{w} \sigma_j{}^2 = \frac{c-1}{2c} \sum_{j=1}^{w} D_j. \tag{43}$

XIV. Conclusion and Problems.

The material presented here has been collected in the hope of helping the cryptanalyst with his decision problems. More on this fundamentally sophisticated subject can be found in "Statistics for Cryptology" and "Probability and the Weighing of Evidence" by I. J. Good. Many papers on specific phases of decisions are to be found in the "Collected Papers of Mathematical Cryptology" or in the "Quarterly Summary" of NSA-34.

Problem: A cipher text autokey is a cipher system in which the next cipher letter is determined by the last cipher letter and the present plain letter. What is the expected digraphic I.C. γ_2 of the cipher text?

Problem: Some cipher machines have a switch which must be thrown one way to encipher and the other way to decipher. The switch reverses the direction of flow of information through the machine. A certain operator inadvertently uses decipher on his machine in preparing a message, and sends it that way. The recipient is unable to understand it and requests a resend. The operator repeats his operation, using the same setting as before, but with the switch now on encipher. You, the cryptanalyst, compare the two texts letter for letter. What comparison I.C. ι do you expect?

APPENDICES

APPENDIX I

The Relation between the Monographic and Digraphic I. C.

The monographic and digraphic I. C.'s are not independent. For if the probabilities of the individual letters are p_1, p_2, – – –, p_c then the expected probability $E(p_{ij})$ of the digraph ij is p_ip_j, ignoring the cohesion of the language, and for the moment imagining a sample like newspaper which has been cut into little pieces, one letter to a piece, which have been shuffled and arranged in a line. Using this estimate of p_{ij} we get the expected value

$$E(\gamma_2) = E\left\{c^2 \sum_{i=1}^{c} \sum_{j=1}^{c} p_{ij}^2\right\} = c^2 \sum_{i=1}^{c} \sum_{j=1}^{c} p_i^2 p_j^2 = c \sum_{i=1}^{c} p_i^2 c \sum_{j=1}^{c} p_j^2 = \gamma^2.$$

It is true however that language does have cohesion and that each letter affects the frequency of occurrence of others in its vicinity. Usually then the digraphic I. C. is in excess of the estimate γ_2 above. We will sometimes calculate the ratio

$$\chi = \frac{\gamma_2}{\gamma^2}$$ and call it the "index of cohesion".

Estimates of the higher I. C.'s can be made in the same way.

One can show that

$$E(\gamma_k) = \gamma_{k-1}\gamma, \text{ or } E(\gamma_k) = \gamma_{kj} - \gamma_j.$$

Differences between these estimates of γ_k will be due to the various kinds of cohesion in the text.

One application of these relations occurs in the analysis of fractionating* systems, where as a preliminary to enciphering the text is expressed as a product of components and each component is enciphered separately, and then the cipher text is recombined into ordinary letters. For instance, each of c = 25 letters may be expressed as a two digit number, where the first digit is 0, 1, 2, 3, or 4 and the second is 5, 6, 7, 8, or 9. The I. C. of the combined text is the product of the I. C.'s of the fractions, as shown by an argument similar to that for digraphs.

*In this connection, the following works will be of interest:

TM 32–220, "Basic Cryptography," Dept. of the Army, April 1950 pp. 155–163

"Military Cryptanalysis, Part IV" by Wm. F. Friedman OCSigO, Washington, 1941, pp. 144–184

"Elementary Cryptanalysis," by Helen F. Gaines, American Photographic Publishing Co., Boston, 1944, pp. 209–212

APPENDIX II

A Proof that the Expected Cross I. C. is 1

As in section VIII the relative frequencies of one text are p_i and those for other are q_i, where $\sum_{i=1}^{c} p_i = 1$ and $\sum_{i=1}^{c} q_i = 1$. We will use $P = c \sum_{i=1}^{c} p_i{}^1$ and $Q = c \sum_{i=1}^{c} q_i{}^1$ for the I.C.'s of the two texts. We wish to predict the value of $\xi = c \sum_{i=1}^{c} p_i q_i$.

To do this we imagine the values of the q_i's permuted among themselves and observe what happens to ξ. That is, we imagine another sample of text replacing the second, a sample for which the frequency numbers are the same but not necessarily for the same letters. The I. C. of the new sample is necessarily the same as that of the original, since the I. C. does not depend on which letters are frequent. The average of the ξ over all possible permutations of the q_i's will be seen to be 1. That is, we will calculate

$E(\xi) = \frac{1}{c!} \sum_p \xi$, where the p under the summation sign means the sum over all the permutations

of the q's, c! in number. Thus

$$E(\xi) = \frac{1}{c!} \sum_p C \sum_{i=1}^{c} p_i q_i{}^1$$

where $q_i{}^1$ is one of the q's, depending on the permutation. Each q will appear with a given subscript i exactly $(c-1)!$ times.

Thus $\sum_p q_i{}^1 = (c-1)! \sum_{i=1}^{c} q_i{}^1 = (c-1)!$,

and $E(\xi) = \frac{c}{c!} \sum_{i=1}^{c} p_i \sum_p q_i{}^1 = \frac{1}{(c-1)!} \sum_{i=1}^{c} p_i (c-1)! = \sum_{i=1}^{c} p_i = 1$.

Notice that this result is independent of the roughness of either distribution.

To find the variance of ξ we evaluate

$$E(\xi^1) = \frac{1}{c!} \sum_p \left(c \sum_{i=1}^{c} p_i q_i \right)^2 = \frac{1}{c!} \sum_p c^2 \sum_{i=1}^{c} \sum_{j=1}^{c} p_i q_i{}^1 p_j q_j{}^1,$$

$$= \frac{c^2}{c!} \sum_{i=1}^{c} \sum_{j=1}^{c} p_i p_j \sum_p q_i{}^1 q_j{}^1$$

The term $\sum_p q_i{}^1 q_j{}^1$ will depend on whether $i \neq j$ or $i = j$. For $i \neq j$ we have

$$\sum_p q_i{}^1 q_j{}^1 = (c-2)! \sum_{i=1}^{c} \sum_{j \neq i} q_i q_j$$

$$= (c-2)! \sum_{i=1}^{c} q_i \sum_{j \neq i} q_j = (c-2)! \sum_{i=1}^{c} q_i (1 - q_i)$$

$$= (c-2)! \left(\sum_{i=1}^{c} q_i - \sum_{i=1}^{c} q_i^2 \right) = (c-2)! \left(1 - \frac{Q}{c} \right).$$

For $i = j$ we have

$$\sum_{p} q_i^2 = (c-1)! \sum_{i=1}^{c} q_i^2 = (c-1)! \frac{Q}{c}.$$

APPENDIX III

The Standard Deviation of the I.C.

1. In Kullback's "Statistical Methods in Cryptanalysis", Appendix D, page 151, the standard deviation of $\phi = \sum_{i=1}^{c} f_i(f_i - 1)$ is derived for a universe with prescribed probabilities p_i. For convenience the abbreviations $S_2 = \sum_{i=1}^{c} p_i^2$, $S_3 = \sum_{i=1}^{c} p_i^3$, and $S_4 = \sum_{i=1}^{c} p_i^4$ are made. The result is then obtained, $\sigma^2(\phi) = 4M^3(S_3 - S_2^2) + 2M^2(-6S_3 + S_2 + 5S_2^2) + 2M(4S_3 - S_2 - 3S_2^2)$.

For the flat universe with $p_i = \frac{1}{c} = p_j$ we have

$$S_2 = \sum_{1}^{c} \frac{1}{c^2} = \frac{1}{c}, \; S_3 = \sum_{1}^{c} \frac{1}{c^3} = \frac{1}{c^2}, \text{ and } \quad S_4 = \sum_{1}^{c} \frac{1}{c^4} = \frac{1}{c^3}. \text{ Then}$$

$$\sigma^2(\phi) = 4M^3\left(\frac{1}{c^2} - \frac{1}{c^2}\right) + 2M^2\left(-\frac{6}{c^2} + \frac{1}{c} + \frac{5}{c^2}\right) + 2M\left(\frac{4}{c^2} - \frac{1}{c} - \frac{3}{c^2}\right)$$

$$= 2M^2\left(\frac{1}{c} - \frac{1}{c^2}\right) + 2M\left(\frac{1}{c^2} - \frac{1}{c}\right) = 2M(M-1)\frac{c-1}{c^2}.$$

The relation between ϕ and δ is that $\delta = \frac{c}{M(M-1)} \sum_{i=1}^{c} f_i(f_i - 1) = \frac{c}{M(M-1)} \phi$.

Therefore $\sigma^2(\delta) = \frac{c^2}{M^2(M-1)^2} \sigma^2(\phi) = \frac{2(c-1)}{M(M-1)}$.

The relation between δ and γ is that $\gamma = \frac{M-1}{M} \delta + \frac{c}{M}$ whence

$$\sigma^2(\gamma) = \left(\frac{M-1}{M}\right)^2 \sigma^2(\delta) = 2\frac{M-1}{M^3}(c-1).$$

2. The comparison IC is $\iota = \frac{g}{N/c}$. The numerator g is binomially distributed with probabilities $p = \frac{1}{c}$ and $q = 1 - \frac{1}{c}$ of success and failure, assuming the random universe. Then $\sigma^2(g) = Npq = N\frac{c-1}{c^2}$. Therefore $\sigma^2(\iota) = \frac{c^2}{N^2} \sigma^2(g) = \frac{c-1}{N}$.

Thus $E(\xi^2) = \frac{c^2}{c!} \sum_{i=1}^{c} p_i \sum_{j \neq 1} p_j(c-2)! \left(1 - \frac{Q}{c}\right) + \frac{c^2}{c!} \sum_{i=1}^{c} p_i^2(c-1)! \frac{Q}{c}$

$$= \frac{c^2}{c!}(c-2)!\left(1 - \frac{Q}{c}\right) \sum_{i=1}^{c} p_i \sum_{j \neq 1} p_j + \frac{c^2}{c!}(c-1)! \frac{Q}{c} \sum_{i=1}^{c} p_i^2$$

$$= \frac{c-Q}{c-1} \sum_{i=1}^{c} p_i(1-p_i) + \frac{QP}{c} \quad = \frac{c-Q}{c-1}\left(1 - \frac{P}{c}\right) + \frac{QP}{c}$$

$$= \frac{(c-Q)(c-P)}{(c-1)c} + \frac{QP}{c} \quad = \frac{c-P-Q+QP}{c-1}$$

33

Now by definition $\sigma^2(\xi) = E(\xi^2) - [E(\xi)]^2$

$$= \frac{c-P-Q+QP}{c-1} - 1 = \frac{1-P-Q+QP}{c-1} = \frac{(P-1)(Q-1)}{c-1}.$$

APPENDIX IV

Proof of the Formula of Section X

The probability p_i of the ith letter occurring in the sum is $p_i = \sum_j q_j r_{i-j}$.

Then $\gamma = c \sum_i p_i{}^2 = c \sum_i \sum_j \sum_k q_j q_k r_{i-j} r_{i-k}$.

We compute the expected value of γ by making all substitutions in turn one of the two streams and averaging the results.

$$E(\gamma) = \frac{c}{c!} \sum_{\substack{perm \\ r}} \sum_i \sum_j \sum_k q_j q_k r_{i-j} r_{i-k} = \frac{c}{c!} \sum_i \sum_j \sum_k q_j q_k \sum_{\substack{perm \\ r}} r_{i-j} r_{i-k}.$$

But $\sum_{\substack{perm \\ r}} r_s r_t = (c-2)! \sum_{s \neq t} \sum r_s r_t = (c-2)!(1 - \sum_s r_s{}^2)$.

Therefore $E(\gamma) = \dfrac{c}{c!} \sum_i \left\{ \sum_j q_j{}^2 \sum_{\substack{perm \\ r}} r_i{}^2 + \sum_{j \neq k} \sum q_j q_k \sum_{\substack{perm \\ r}} r_{i-j} r_{i-k} \right\}$

$= \dfrac{c^2}{c!} \left\{ (c-1)! \sum_j q_j{}^2 \sum_t r_t{}^2 + (1 - \sum_j q_j{}^2)(1 - \sum_k r_k{}^2)(c-2)! \right\}$

$= \dfrac{c}{c-1} \left\{ (c-1) \dfrac{\gamma_1}{c} \dfrac{\gamma_2}{c} + 1 - \dfrac{\gamma_1}{c} - \dfrac{\gamma_2}{c} + \dfrac{\gamma_1 \gamma_2}{c^2} \right\}$

$= \dfrac{1}{c-1} \left\{ (c-1) \dfrac{\gamma_1 \gamma_2}{c} + c - \gamma_1 - \gamma_2 + \dfrac{\gamma_1 \gamma_2}{c} \right\}$

$= \dfrac{1}{c-1} \left\{ \gamma_1 \gamma_2 - \gamma_1 - \gamma_2 + c \right\} = \dfrac{(\gamma_1 - 1)(\gamma_2 - 1)}{c-1} + \dfrac{c-1}{c-1} = 1 + \dfrac{\beta_1 \beta_2}{c-1}$

APPENDIX V

Proof of the Mixture Formula

We have assumed k sources of text, each with its own frequency distribution. Suppose the ith distribution to be $p_{i1}, p_{i2}, p_{i3}, \cdots$ with $\beta_i = c \sum_{j=1} p_{ij}^2 - 1$, $i = 1, 2, \cdots, k$.

Suppose that the relative proportions that the k sources are used are $r_1 : r_2 : \ldots : r_k$ with $\sum_1^k r_i = 1$.

Then if q_j is the proportion of a letter in the resulting mixture, $q_j = r_1 p_{1j} + r_2 p_{2j} + \ldots + r_k p_{kj}$.

The I.C. of the mixture is

$$\gamma = c \sum_{j=1}^c q_j^2 = c \sum_{j=1}^c \left(\sum_{i=1}^k r_i p_{ij} \right)^2 = c \sum_{j=1}^c \sum_{i=1}^k \sum_{h=1}^k r_i r_h p_{ij} p_{hj}.$$

$$= \sum_{i=1}^k \sum_{h=1}^k r_i r_h c \sum_{j=1}^c p_{ij} p_{hj} = \sum_{i=1}^k \sum_{h=1}^k r_i r_h \xi_{ih}$$

where $\xi_{ih} = c \sum_{j=1}^c p_{ij} p_{hj}$ is the cross I.C. of the ith and hth sources. The special case $\xi_{ii} = \gamma_i$ is the I.C. of the ith source.

Now the I.C. becomes $\gamma = \sum_{i=1}^k \sum_{h \neq i} r_i r_h \xi_{ih} + \sum_{i=1}^k r_i^2 \gamma_i$.

If the k sources are unrelated then $E(\xi_{ih}) = 1$ and we have

$$E(\gamma) = \sum_{i=1}^k \sum_{h \neq 1} r_i r_h + \sum_{i=1}^k r_i \gamma_i = \sum_{i=1}^k \sum_{h \neq i} r_i r_h + \sum_{i=1}^k r_i^2 (1 + \gamma_i - 1)$$

$$= \sum_{i=1}^k \sum_{h=1}^k r_i r_h + \sum_{i=1}^k r_i^2 \beta_i$$

where $\beta_i = \gamma_i - 1$ is the bulge. In this last algebraic manipulation we have removed the restriction on the range of the summation index h by changing from I.C. to bulge. Without the restriction we have $\sum_{i=1}^k \sum_{h=1}^k r_i r_h = \sum_{i=1}^k \gamma_i \sum_{h=1}^k r_h = 1$ so that $E(\beta) = E(\gamma) - 1 = \sum_{i=1}^k r_i^2 \beta_i$.

APPENDIX VI

I. C. DISTRIBUTION AND TABLES

1. Distribution of the γ or δ I. C.   (χ^2 method).
2. Distribution of the Cross I. C.
3. Distribution of ι I. C.
4. Tables of I. C.
5. Short Cumulative Poisson Table
6. Short Table of Logarithms of Factorials

1. **Distribution of the γ or δ I. C.   (χ^2 method).**

If we have a frequency count $f_1, f_2, ---, f_c$ in a c letter alphabet where

$$\sum_{i=1}^{c} f_i = N, \text{ then}$$

$$\chi^2 = \frac{c}{N}\sum_{i=1}^{c}\left(f_i - \frac{N}{c}\right)^2 = N(\gamma - 1), \text{ where } \gamma = \frac{c}{N^2}\sum_{i=1}^{c} f_i^2 \text{ is the } \gamma \text{ I.C.}$$

The distribution of χ^2 is known **asymptotically**.   This case has $c-1$ degrees of freedom.

$$P(\gamma \leq X) = P(\chi^2 \leq N[X-1])$$

$$= \frac{2^{\frac{1-c}{2}}}{\Gamma\left(\frac{c-1}{2}\right)} \int_0^{N(X-1)} t^{\frac{c-3}{2}} e^{\frac{t}{2}} dt \quad \text{(See Cramer p. 234.)}$$

$$= \frac{1}{\Gamma\left(\frac{c-1}{2}\right)} \int_0^{N\left(\frac{X-1}{2}\right)} u^{\frac{c-3}{2}} e^{-u} du$$

$$= \frac{\Gamma_{N\frac{X-1}{2}}\left(\frac{c-1}{2}\right)}{\Gamma\left(\frac{c-1}{2}\right)}$$

$$= I\left(N\frac{(X-1)}{2}, \frac{c-3}{2}\right)$$

$$E(\gamma) = 1 + \frac{c-1}{N} = \gamma_0.$$

$$\sigma = \sigma(\gamma) = \sqrt{\frac{2(c-1)}{N^2}}$$

Let $S = \frac{\gamma - \gamma_0}{\sigma} = \frac{\gamma - 1 - \frac{c-1}{N}}{\sqrt{\frac{2(c-1)}{N}}} = \frac{N(\gamma-1)-c+1}{\sqrt{2(c-1)}}$

Then $P(S \leq S_0) = P(\gamma \leq \gamma_0 + S_0\sigma)$

$$= P\left(\gamma \leq 1 + \frac{c-1}{N} + S_0\frac{\sqrt{2(c-1)}}{N}\right)$$

$$= \frac{\Gamma_{\frac{c-1+S_0\sqrt{2(c-1)}}{2}}\left(\frac{c-1}{2}\right)}{\Gamma\frac{(c-1)}{2}}$$

$$= I\left(\frac{c-1}{2}+S_0\sqrt{\frac{c-1}{2}}, \frac{c-3}{2}\right)$$

If we take $\frac{N}{N-1} \doteq 1$ (Error less than 1% for $N \geq 50$). The above is reasonably accurate and can be tabulated for values of sigmage S without regard for sample size.

Values for the above are tabulated by translation from Pearson's Tables of the Incomplete Gamma Function.

In addition,

$$\delta = \gamma\frac{c-\gamma}{N-1} = \left(\frac{N}{N-1}\right)\gamma - \left(\frac{c}{N-1}\right).$$

For each particular δ_0 we get a corresponding γ_0 such that

$$\delta_0 = \left(\frac{N}{N-1}\right)\gamma_0 - \left(\frac{c}{N-1}\right) \quad \text{or} \quad \gamma_0 = \frac{\delta_0(N-1)-c}{N}.$$

Notice that

$$P(\delta \leq \delta_0) = P\left(\frac{N}{N-1}\gamma - \frac{c}{N-1} \leq \frac{N}{N-1}\gamma_0 - \frac{c}{N-1}\right),$$

and this is merely $P(\gamma \leq \gamma_0)$.

Therefore the table is valid for δ as well as γ.

As a rough rule of thumb these tables are applicable if each category has more than 5 tallies.

2. Distribution of the Cross I. C.

The cross I.C. ξ is a measure of the fit between two frequency counts. Let one of these be f_i and the other g_i, with $\sum_{i=1}^{c} f_i = M$ and $\sum_{i=1}^{c} g_i = N$ and $c =$ the number of letters in the alphabet.

Then $\xi = \frac{c\Sigma f_i g_i}{MN}$.

Let $P = \frac{c\Sigma f_i^2}{M^2}$ and $Q = \frac{c\Sigma g_i^2}{N^2}$ be the I.C.'s.

Then $\sigma^2(\xi) = \frac{(P-1)(Q-1)}{c-1}$ is the variance, and

$$S(\xi) = \frac{\xi - 1}{\sigma} = \frac{(\xi - 1)\sqrt{c-1}}{\sqrt{(P-1)(Q-1)}} \text{ is the sigmage.}$$

The distribution of $S(\xi)$ has the fortunate property of being approximately independent of the sample size. This makes it feasible to tabulate its distribution.

The table, each entry of which is the probability of getting a certain sigmage or higher, was made by translating from Pearson's Table of the Incomplete Beta Function by the formula

$$P[S(\xi) \geq k] = I_{\frac{1 - \frac{k}{\sqrt{c-1}}}{2}}\left(\frac{c-2}{2}, \frac{c-2}{2}\right).$$

See series of reports on Gleason's "Distribution of the Correlation Coefficient".

3. Distribution of ι I. C.

$$\iota = \frac{ch}{N}$$

where

h = Number of hits,

N = Amount of overlap.

c = Number of categories (letters in alphabet),

and

p = $1/c$ = Probability of individual hit occurring.

The distribution of ι is exactly binomial, and

$$P(h = X) = \binom{N}{X} \frac{1}{c^N} (c-1)^{N-X}$$

Then

$$P(h \geq X) = \frac{1}{c^N} \sum_{j=X}^{N} \binom{N}{j} (c-1)^{N-j},$$

and

$$P(\iota \geq k) = P\left(h \geq \frac{Nk}{c}\right) = \frac{1}{c^N} \sum_{j=\frac{Nk}{c}}^{N} \binom{N}{j} (c-1)^{N-j}$$

Values for this can be found in appropriate binomial distribution tables with $n = N$, $r = \frac{Nk}{c}$

and $p = \frac{1}{c}$.

These values can be very well approximated for cases where $N > 10c$ by entering Poisson Table II with $a = \frac{N}{c}$, $X = k$.

Tables for the distribution of ι are therefore not presented herein.

ORIGINAL

k	Normal $P(S \geq k)$	Cross I. C. $P[S(\xi) \geq k]$				Gamma I. C. $P[S(\gamma) \geq k]$			
		C = 10	C = 26	C = 30	C = 32	C = 10	C = 15	C = 17	C = 19
00.0	.5000	.500	.500	.500	.500	.437	.450	.453	.456
00.1	.460	.464	.461	.462	.461	.399	.411	.414	.417
00.2	.421	.427	.423	.421	.423	.363	.374	.377	.380
00.3	.382	.392	.385	.384	.385	.329	.339	.342	.344
00.4	.345	.357	.349	.349	.348	.297	.307	.309	.311
00.5	.308	.323	.313	.315	.312	.268	.276	.278	.279
00.6	.274	.290	.280	.278	.248	.240	.247	.249	.250
00.7	.242	.258	.248	.247	.246	.215	.221	.222	.223
00.8	.212	.228	.217	.218	.216	.192	.197	.198	.198
00.9	.184	.200	.189	.188	.188	.171	.174	.175	.176
01.0	.159	.173	.164	.168	.162	.152	.154	.155	.155
01.1	.136	.149	.140	.140	.139	.135	.136	.136	.136
01.2	.115	.126	.119	.119	.118	.119	.120	.120	.120
01.3	.0968	.106	.100	.0989	.0990	.105	.105	.105	.104
01.4	.0808	.0871	.0830	.0826	.0824	.0927	.0918	.0914	.0910
01.5	.0668	.0706	.0682	.0686	.0678	.0815	.0801	.0796	.0790
01.6	.0548	.0563	.0555	.0550	.0552	.0715	.0697	.0691	.0684
01.7	.0446	.0439	.0446	.0446	.0445	.0627	.0605	.0598	.0591
01.8	.0359	.0333	.0354	.0358	.0354	.0548	.0524	.0516	.0509
01.9	.0287	.0247	.0278	.0284	.0278	.0478	.0452	.0445	.0437
02.0	.0228	.0177	.0214	.0216	.0215	.0417	.0390	.0382	.0374
02.1	.0179	.0121	.0163	.0167	.0165	.0363	.0336	.0328	.0320
02.2	.0139	.00795	.0122	.0127	.0125	.0315	.0288	.0280	.0273
02.3	.0107	.00488	.00903	.00925	.00934	.0274	.0247	.0239	.0282
02.4	.0082	.00273	.00654	.00682	.00711	.0237	.0211	.0204	.0197
02.5	.0062	.00140	.00465	.00494	.00514	.0205	.0180	.0173	.0167
02.6	.0047	.000602	.00324	.00351	.00364	.0178	.0153	.0147	.0141
02.7	.0035	.000194	.00220	.00237	.00253	.0153	.0131	.0124	.0119
02.8	.0026	.0000447	.00146	.00161	.00172	.0132	.0111	.0105	.0100
02.9	.0019	.0000037	.000949	.00109	.00118	.0114	.00941	.00888	.00841

k	Gamma I. C. $P[S(\gamma) \geq k]$								
	C = 20	C = 21	C = 23	C = 25	C = 26	C = 30	C = 32	C = 35	C = 40
00.0	.457	.458	.459	.462	.463	.465	.466	.468	.469
00.1	.418	.419	.421	.423	.424	.426	.427	.429	.431
00.2	.381	.382	.384	.385	.386	.388	.389	.391	.393
00.3	.345	.346	.348	.349	.350	.352	.353	.355	.356
00.4	.312	.313	.314	.315	.316	.318	.319	.320	.322
00.5	.280	.281	.282	.284	.284	.286	.287	.287	.289
00.6	.251	.252	.253	.254	.254	.255	.256	.257	.258
00.7	.224	.224	.225	.226	.226	.227	.228	.229	.230
00.8	.199	.199	.200	.201	.201	.202	.202	.203	.203
00.9	.176	.176	.177	.177	.178	.178	.078	.179	.179
01.0	.155	.156	.156	.156	.156	.156	.157	.157	.157
01.1	.137	.137	.137	.137	.137	.137	.137	.137	.137
01.2	.120	.120	.120	.120	.120	.119	.119	.119	.119
01.3	.104	.104	.104	.104	.104	.104	.104	.103	.103
01.4	.0909	.0908	.0905	.0903	.0902	.0897	.0896	.0893	.0889
01.5	.0789	.0788	.0784	.0781	.0780	.0773	.0772	.0768	.0763
01.6	.0688	.0681	.0676	.0673	.0671	.0664	.0662	.0658	.0652
01.7	.0589	.0587	.0582	.0578	.0576	.0568	.0566	.0562	.0555
01.8	.0507	.0504	.0499	.0495	.0493	.0485	.0482	.0478	.0471
01.9	.0435	.0432	.0427	.0423	.0420	.0412	.0410	.0405	.0398
02.0	.0372	.0370	.0364	.0360	.0358	.0349	.0347	.0342	.0335
02.1	.0318	.0315	.0309	.0305	.0303	.0295	.0292	.0288	.0281
02.2	.0270	.0268	.0262	.0258	.0256	.0248	.0246	.0241	.0235
02.3	.0230	.0227	.0222	.0218	.0216	.0209	.0206	.0202	.0196
02.4	.0195	.0192	.0187	.0184	.0182	.0175	.0172	.0168	.0163
02.5	.0165	.0162	.0158	.0154	.0152	.0146	.0143	.0140	.0135
02.6	.0139	.0137	.0132	.0129	.0127	.0121	.0119	.0116	.0111
02.7	.0117	.0115	.0111	.0108	.0106	.0101	.00988	.00956	.00914
02.8	.00983	.00964	.00928	.00899	.00885	.00834	.00816	.00788	.00749
02.9	.00824	.00807	.00774	.00747	.00735	.00689	.00672	.00647	.00612

46

k	Normal $P(S \geq k)$	Cross I. C. $P[S(\xi) \geq k]$				Gamma I. C. $P[S(\gamma) \geq k]$			
		C=10	C=26	C=30	C=32	C=10	C=15	C=17	C=19
03.0	.00135	--------	.000597	.000684	.000754	.00980	.00797	.00748	.00706
03.1	--------	--------	.000365	.000441	.000486	.00842	.00673	.00629	.00591
03.2	.00069	--------	.000215	.000277	.000305	.00723	.00568	.00528	.00493
03.3	--------	--------	.000122	.000169	.000186	.00621	.00479	.00443	.00412
03.4	.00034	--------	.0000663	.0000985	.000109	.00532	.00408	.00370	.00343
03.5	--------	--------	.0000344	.0000581	.0000621	.00455	.00339	.00309	.00285
03.6	.00016	--------	.0000169	.0000289	.0000339	.00390	.00284	.00258	.00237
03.7	--------	--------	.0000078	.0000141	.0000177	.00333	.00238	.00215	.00196
03.8	.00007	--------	.0000033	.0000069	.0000088	.00284	.00200	.00179	.00162
03.9	--------	--------	.0000013	.0000032	.0000041	.00243	.00167	.00149	.00134
04.0	.00003	--------	.0000005	.0000014	.0000019	.00207	.00139	.00123	.00111
04.1	--------	--------	.0000001	.0000006	.0000008	.00176	.00116	.00102	.000911
04.2	.0000134	--------	--------	.0000002	.0000007	.00150	.000970	.000847	.000750
04.3	.0000086	--------	--------	.0000001	.0000001	.00128	.000807	.000700	.000616
04.4	.0000055	--------	--------	--------	--------	.00109	.000671	.000579	.000506
04.5	.0000035	--------	--------	--------	--------	.000923	.000558	.000477	.000414
04.6	.0000022	--------	--------	--------	--------	.000783	.000463	.000393	.000339
04.7	.0000014	--------	--------	--------	--------	.000664	.000384	.000324	.000277
04.8	.0000008	--------	--------	--------	--------	.000564	.000318	.000266	.000227
04.9	.0000005	--------	--------	--------	--------	.000477	.000263	.000219	.000185
05.0	.0000002	--------	--------	--------	--------	.000405	.000217	.000179	.000151
05.1	.0000001	--------	--------	--------	--------	.000342	.000180	.000147	.000123
05.2	.0000001	--------	--------	--------	--------	.000290	.000148	.000120	.0000996
05.3	.0000001	--------	--------	--------	--------	.000245	.000122	.0000984	.0000809
05.4	.0000000	--------	--------	--------	--------	.000207	.000101	.0000804	.0000657
05.5	--------	--------	--------	--------	--------	.000175	.0000828	.0000657	.0000532
05.6	--------	--------	--------	--------	--------	.000147	.0000682	.0000535	.0000431
05.7	--------	--------	--------	--------	--------	.000124	.0000560	.0000437	.0000349
05.8	--------	--------	--------	--------	--------	.000105	.0000460	.0000355	.0000282
05.9	--------	--------	--------	--------	--------	.0000884	.0000377	.0000289	.0000227

47

ORIGINAL

k	Gamma I. C. $P[S(\gamma) \geq k]$								
	C=20	C=21	C=23	C=25	C=26	C=30	C=32	C=35	C=40
03.0	.00690	.00674	.00644	.00620	.00609	.00568	.00553	.00530	.00499
03.1	.00576	.00562	.00535	.00513	.00503	.00467	.00453	.00433	.00406
03.2	.00480	.00468	.00444	.00424	.00415	.00383	.00371	.00353	.00329
03.3	.00400	.00389	.00367	.00350	.00342	.00313	.00302	.00287	.00266
03.4	.00332	.00322	.00303	.00288	.00280	.00255	.00246	.00232	.00214
03.5	.00276	.00267	.00250	.00236	.00230	.00208	.00200	.00188	.00172
03.6	.00228	.00220	.00205	.00194	.00188	.00169	.00162	.00152	.00138
03.7	.00189	.00182	.00169	.00158	.00154	.00137	.00131	.00122	.00110
03.8	.00156	.00150	.00138	.00129	.00125	.00111	.00106	.000981	.000381
03.9	.00128	.00123	.00113	.00105	.00102	.000895	.000850	.000786	.000702
04.0	.00106	.00101	.000925	.000857	.000826	.000721	.000683	.000628	.000557
04.1	.000868	.000828	.000754	.000696	.000670	.000580	.000547	.000501	.000442
04.2	.000712	.000677	.000614	.000564	.000542	.000466	.000438	.000399	.000349
04.3	.000584	.000554	.000500	.000457	.000438	.000373	.000350	.000317	.000275
04.4	.000478	.000452	.000406	.000369	.000353	.000299	.000279	.000252	.000217
04.5	.000390	.000368	.000329	.000298	.000284	.000239	.000222	.000199	.000170
04.6	.000319	.000300	.000266	.000240	.000228	.000190	.000176	.000157	.000133
04.7	.000260	.000244	.000215	.000193	.000183	.000151	.000140	.000124	.000104
04.8	.000212	.000198	.000174	.000155	.000147	.000120	.000110	.0000976	.0000814
04.9	.000172	.000160	.000140	.000125	.000118	.0000954	.0000872	.0000767	.0000635
05.0	.000140	.000130	.000113	.0000997	.0000939	.0000754	.0000688	.0000602	.0000494
05.1	.000113	.000105	.0000907	.0000797	.0000750	.0000596	.0000541	.0000470	.0000383
05.2	.0000919	.0000849	.0000729	.0000636	.0000597	.0000471	.0000427	.0000368	.0000297
05.3	.0000743	.0000685	.0000584	.0000509	.0000476	.0000370	.0000335	.0000287	.0000229
05.4	.0000601	.0000552	.0000469	.0000405	.0000378	.0000292	.0000263	.0000223	.0000177
05.5	.0000484	.0000444	.0000375	.0000322	.0000300	.0000229	.0000206	.0000174	.0000136
05.6	.0000392	.0000358	.0000299	.0000256	.0000238	.0000181	.0000161	.0000134	.0000106
05.7	.0000316	.0000287	.0000240	.0000203	.0000188	.0000141	.0000125	.0000105	.0000080
06.8	.0000255	.0000230	.0000190	.0000161	.0000149	.0000111	.0000098	.0000080	.0000061
05.9	.0000204	.0000185	.0000152	.0000128	.0000118	.0000087	.0000076	.0000063	.0000047

k	Normal P(S≥k)	Cross I. C. P[S(ξ)≥k]				Gamma I. C. P[S(γ)≥k]			
		C=10	C=26	C=80	C=32	C=10	C=15	C=17	C=19
06.0	--------	--------	--------	--------	--------	.0000746	.0000810	.0000235	.0000184
06.1	--------	--------	--------	--------	--------	.0000628	.0000254	.0000192	.0000148
06.2	--------	--------	--------	--------	--------	.0000528	.0000208	.0000155	.0000119
06.3	--------	--------	--------	--------	--------	.0000444	.0000170	.0000126	.0000096
06.4	--------	--------	--------	--------	--------	.0000373	.0000139	.0000102	.0000077
06.5	--------	--------	--------	--------	--------	.0000814	.0000113	.0000082	.0000062
06.6	--------	--------	--------	--------	--------	.0000264	.0000093	.0000067	.0000050
06.7	--------	--------	--------	--------	--------	.0000221	.0000076	.0000054	.0000040
06.8	--------	--------	--------	--------	--------	.0000185	.0000062	.0000044	.0000032
06.9	--------	--------	--------	--------	--------	.0000156	.0000051	.0000035	.0000026
07.0	--------	--------	--------	--------	--------	.0000131	.0000041	.0000028	.0000020
07.1	--------	--------	--------	--------	--------	.0000110	.0000084	.0000023	.0000016
07.2	--------	--------	--------	--------	--------	.0000092	.0000027	.0000019	.0000013
07.3	--------	--------	--------	--------	--------	.0000076	.0000022	.0000015	.0000010
07.4	--------	--------	--------	--------	--------	.0000065	.0000018	.0000012	.0000008
07.5	--------	--------	--------	--------	--------	.0000054	.0000015	.0000009	.0000007
07.6	--------	--------	--------	--------	--------	.0000045	.0000012	.0000008	.0000005
07.7	--------	--------	--------	--------	--------	.0000038	.0000010	.0000006	.0000004
07.8	--------	--------	--------	--------	--------	.0000032	.0000008	.0000005	.0000003
07.9	--------	--------	--------	--------	--------	.0000027	.0000007	.0000004	.0000003
08.0	--------	--------	--------	--------	--------	.0000022	.0000005	.0000008	.0000002
08.1	--------	--------	--------	--------	--------	.0000020	.0000005	.0000008	.0000002
08.2	--------	--------	--------	--------	--------	.0000016	.0000003	.0000002	.0000001
08.3	--------	--------	--------	--------	--------	.0000014	.0000003	.0000001	.0000001
08.4	--------	--------	--------	--------	--------	.0000011	.0000002	.0000001	.0000001
08.5	--------	--------	--------	--------	--------	.0000010	.0000002	.0000001	.0000001
08.6	--------	--------	--------	--------	--------	.0000007	.0000001	.0000001	--------
08.7	--------	--------	--------	--------	--------	.0000007	.0000001	.0000001	....
08.8	--------	--------	--------	--------	--------	.0000006	.0000001	.0000001	....
08.9	--------	--------	--------	--------	--------	.0000005	.0000001	------	--------

k	Gamma I. C. $P[S(\gamma) \geq k]$								
	C = 20	C = 21	C = 23	C = 25	C = 26	C = 30	C = 32	C = 35	C = 40
06.0	.0000165	.0000148	.0000121	.0000101	.0000093	.0000067	.0000058	.0000048	.0000036
06.1	.0000132	.0000118	.0000096	.0000080	.0000073	.0000053	.0000045	.0000037	.0000028
06.2	.0000105	.0000095	.0000076	.0000063	.0000058	.0000040	.0000035	.0000028	.0000020
06.3	.0000085	.0000076	.0000061	.0000050	.0000045	.0000032	.0000026	.0000022	.0000016
06.4	.0000068	.0000060	.0000048	.0000039	.0000036	.0000026	.0000021	.0000017	.0000012
06.5	.0000055	.0000048	.0000088	.0000031	.0000028	.0000020	.0000018	.0000014	.0000010
06.6	.0000044	.0000039	.0000030	.0000024	.0000021	.0000014	.0000012	.0000010	.0000006
06.7	.0000036	.0000030	.0000024	.0000019	.0000017	.0000012	.0000008	.0000007	.0000005
06.8	.0000028	.0000025	.0000018	.0000015	.0000014	.0000008	.0000008	.0000006	.0000004
06.9	.0000022	.0000019	.0000015	.0000012	.0000012	.0000006	.0000006	.0000006	.0000002
07.0	.0000018	.0000016	.0000012	.0000009	.0000008	.0000004	.0000006	.0000004	.0000002
07.1	.0000015	.0000012	.0000009	.0000007	.0000006	.0000004	.0000004	.0000002	.0000002
07.2	.0000012	.0000010	.0000008	.0000006	.0000006	.0000002	.0000002	.0000002	.0000000
07.3	.0000010	.0000007	.0000006	.0000005	.0000004	.0000002	.0000002	.0000002	--------
07.4	.0000008	.0000007	.0000005	.0000003	.0000002	.0000002	.0000002	.0000001	--------
07.5	.0000006	.0000004	.0000003	.0000002	.0000002	.0000002	.0000000	.0000001	--------
07.6	.0000004	.0000004	.0000003	.0000002	.0000002	.0000000	--------	.0000001	--------
07.7	.0000002	.0000003	.0000002	.0000002	.0000002	--------	--------	.0000001	--------
07.8	.0000002	.0000002	.0000002	.0000001	.0000000	--------	--------	--------	--------
07.9	.0000002	.0000002	.0000001	.0000001	--------	--------	--------	--------	--------
08.0	.0000002	.0000002	.0000001	.0000001	--------	--------	--------	--------	--------
08.1	.0000000	.0000001	.0000001	.0000001	--------	--------	--------	--------	--------
08.2	--------	.0000001	.0000001	.0000001	--------	--------	--------	--------	--------
08.3	--------	.0000001	.0000001	--------	--------	--------	--------	--------	--------
08.4	--------	.0000001	--------	--------	--------	--------	--------	--------	--------
08.5	--------	.0000001	--------	--------	--------	--------	--------	--------	--------
08.6	--------	--------	--------	--------	--------	--------	--------	--------	--------
08.7	--------	--------	--------	--------	--------	--------	--------	--------	--------
08.8	--------	--------	--------	--------	--------	--------	--------	--------	--------
08.9	--------	--------	--------	--------	--------	--------	--------	--------	--------

k	Normal $P(S \geq k)$	Cross I. C. $P[S(\xi) \geq k]$				Gamma I. C. $P[S(\gamma) \geq k]$			
		C=10	C=26	C=30	C=32	C=10	C=15	C=17	C=19
09.0	--------	--------	--------	--------	--------	.0000004	.0000001	--------	--------
09.1	--------	--------	--------	--------	--------	.0000003	.0000001	--------	--------
09.2	--------	--------	--------	--------	--------	.0000002	--------	--------	--------
09.3	--------	--------	--------	--------	--------	.0000002	--------	--------	--------
09.4	--------	--------	--------	--------	--------	.0000002	--------	--------	--------
09.5	--------	--------	--------	--------	--------	.0000002	--------	--------	--------
09.6	--------	--------	--------	--------	--------	.0000001	--------	--------	--------
09.7	--------	--------	--------	--------	--------	.0000001	--------	--------	--------
09.8	--------	--------	--------	--------	--------	.0000001	--------	--------	--------
09.0	--------	--------	--------	--------	--------	.0000001	--------	--------	--------
10.0	--------	--------	--------	--------	--------	.0000001	--------	--------	--------
10.1	--------	--------	--------	--------	--------	.0000001	--------	--------	--------
10.2	--------	--------	--------	--------	--------	--------	--------	--------	--------

5. Short Cumulative Poisson Table P(x,a).

a / x	5	7	10	12	13	15	17	20
5	.56	.83	.971	.9924	.9963	.99914	.99982	.99983
6	.38	.70	.933	.980				
7	.24	.55	.87	.954	.974	.9924	.9979	.99975
8	.13	.40	.78	.910				
9	.068	.27	.67	.841	.900	.963	.987	.9979
10	.032	.17	.54	.76				
11	.014	.10	.42	.65	.75	.88	.951	.989
12	.055	.053	.30	.54				
13	.0020	.027	.21	.42	.54	.73	.86	.961
14	.00070	.013	.14	.32				
15	.00023	.0057	.083	.23	.32	.53	.72	.895
16	.000069	.0024	.049	.16				
17	.000020	.00096	.027	.10	.16	.36	.53	.78
18	.000005	.00036	.014	.063				
19	.000001	.00013	.0072	.037	.070	.18	.35	.62
20		.000044	.0035	.021				.53
21		.000014	.0016	.012	.025	.083	.19	.44
22		.000005	.00070	.0061				
23		.000001	.00030	.0030	.0076	.033	.095	.28
24			.00012	.0015				
25			.000047	.00069	.0020	.011	.041	.16
26			.000018	.00031				
27			.000006	.00013	.00045	.0033	.015	.078
28			.000002	.000056				
29			.000001	.000023	.000089	.00086	.0050	.034
30				.000009				

6. Short Table of Logarithms of Factorials.

N	log N!	N	log N!
2	.30	100	158
3	.78	200	375
4	1.4	300	614
5	2.1	400	868
6	2.9	500	1134
7	3.7	600	1408
8	4.6	676	1621
9	5.6	700	1689
10	6.6	800	1977
20	18.4	900	2270
26	26.6	1000	2568
30	32.4	1024	2640
32	35.4	2000	5736
36	41.6	3000	9131
40	47.9	4000	12673
50	64.5	5000	16326
60	81.9		
70	100.		
80	119.		
90	138.